TOTTENHAM HOTSPUR GREATS

TOTTENHAM HOTSPUR GREATS

Harry Harris

Foreword by
Irving Scholar

SPORTSPRINT PUBLISHING
EDINBURGH

ISBN 0 85976 309 9

British Library Cataloguing in Publication Data
Harris, Harry *1952-*
  Tottenham Hotspur greats.
  1. England. Association football. Clubs. Tottenham Hotspur
Football Club, history
  I. Title
  796.334630942188

Phototypeset by Beecee Typesetting Services
Printed in Great Britain by Bell & Bain Ltd., Glasgow

Foreword

Any book about Tottenham Hotspur Football Club is a labour of love.

To try to choose one's own selection of the greatest ever players is a nigh impossible task.

Being a follower of Spurs, one never fully appreciates how lucky we have been to have watched so many outstanding players in our colours.

Older followers talk in awe of players such as Dimmock, O'Callaghan, Seed, whilst in more modern times, supporters drool over the exploits of wonderful players such as Hoddle, Ardiles and Waddle.

Football is the most talked about sport on this planet, and nothing provokes stronger debate than when people choose their greatest ever players.

Who is to say that the late great John White was better than Ossie Ardiles? Or whether Cliff Jones was a finer winger than Chris Waddle? Or whether Glenn Hoddle was a better passer of the ball than Danny Blanchflower?

One thing is for sure: Jimmy Greaves was the greatest ever goalscorer to play with the Cockerel on his heart.

I'm sure this book will provoke even more discussion, but in the end every supporter has his own particular favourite choices.

The author Harry Harris is very well qualified, having always been a Spurs follower in his youth and into his professional life.

I am pleased to see that he has included my personal favourite choice, whom I idolised as a young supporter, a centre forward with magnificent skills, guile and sheer class. A description that could so easily fit so many players who have graced the club.

Irving Scholar,
Chairman

v

Acknowledgements

I am indebted to Len Greener, Picture Editor of the *Daily Mirror*, for his kind permission to raid the comprehensive Mirror Group Newspaper Library for photographs used in this book, and my good friend and colleague Siggy Jacobsen for his painstaking efforts in choosing the right ones!

I must also thank Spurs chairman Irving Scholar for his Foreword. He is a genuine Spurs lover and I firmly believe that his enthusiasm for the club is unequalled by any other chairman anywhere in the land.

Of course, no book about Spurs can be written without reference to Bill Nicholson. His book, *Glory, Glory, My Life With Spurs*, is the Spurs followers' 'bible' as being the authoritative voice from the most successful period in the club's history.

Contents

CHAPTER 1

Introduction

To SELECT THE TOP TEN TOTTENHAM GREATS has been the most difficult task I've ever undertaken.

A pleasant task nonetheless.

For I must confess a deep affection for Spurs. I have supported the club since I was old enough to kick a football.

Now, I feel almost privileged to be among their 12,000 individual shareholders, taking the opportunity to buy my tiny corner of the club when they took the initiative to be floated, the first to be listed on the Stock Exchange.

It's with enormous pride that I hold my Tottenham shares. I can join the commuters examining the FT Share Index to see how my 'investment' is getting on.

The truth is that I would never part with those shares, irrespective of the offer.

Not that those shares make the task of sorting out the best players in the club's history any easier!

After many sleepless nights, hours of deliberation, I've finally whittled down my selection.

It's with great respect for the glory, glory days of the past that my selection inevitably concentrates on the '50s, the '60s in particular, and the '70s and early '80s.

The astonishing quality of those players from the past means that there is no room for the current generation led by Paul Gascoigne, Gary Lineker, and skipper Gary Mabbutt — all three outstanding individuals would walk into most other all-time great teams.

Gazza has been a Tottenham player for only two years,

1

Lineker for just one season. Whatever Lineker's phenomenal achievements with Leicester, Everton, Barcelona and England, they cannot qualify in the final analysis regarding Tottenham.

Gazza returned from England's World Cup in Italy a national hero. He departed for the World Cup campaign a £2 million player, and returned to be valued at SIX times that amount. He also won the hearts of the nation for the tears of sorrow he shed as England were cruelly eliminated from the semi-finals on a penalty shoot-out against West Germany. His agony was intensified by a yellow card that would have ruled him out of the Final had England made it.

There is no doubt that Gazza will, very shortly, earn the right to inclusion in the Tottenham Top Ten . . . and for that reason, I dedicate a chapter to young Gazza as a member elect to the special band of Spurs stars.

Personally, I take great pride in the fact that I campaigned vigorously for Gazza's inclusion in the England team, as Bobby Robson will surely testify, not only publicly through my column in the *Daily Mirror* but also privately to the England manager until he was sick of it.

For the moment, for all his midfield ability, despite the fact that he is worth more than the £8 million Juventus paid Fiorentina for Roberto Baggio, I cannot put Gazza ahead of Glenn Hoddle, Ossie Ardiles, Dave Mackay or Danny Blanchflower.

Gazza may have achieved more in a shorter space of time for England, but he has yet to attain really great heights for Spurs. I am sure he will do.

I met Danny Blanchflower at a Double team reunion not so long ago. Now a virtual recluse, this was a rare night out for him. It was not a public appearance, just an informal get-together with his old pals from the 1961 Double side at a Piccadilly club. Maybe the old rapid-fire speech and wit have gone with the passage of time, but once he spotted a face he can trust he is still as eager as ever to talk about the game. During his brief flirtation with soccer management at Chelsea I spent hours on a Sunday afternoon discussing the game with Danny.

His views are no longer as authoritative as they once were, as he confines himself to watching the game on TV, but his opinions are nonetheless fascinating. He had the foresight to tell me long before the World Cup: 'Gascoigne has some good qualities but he has to become a team player. Perhaps he needs to get the right players around him.

'I don't go to football anymore, but I watch it on television, and I'm afraid the game is no longer a sport for me, it's too much money-orientated, a business . . . no-one is worth £2 million.

'If he wants to be an outstanding player, Gazza must learn to link up with the players ahead of him, or to understand when space is being created for him to move into.

'I'm also afraid that opponents are putting the boot in, they have no intention of letting him play, letting him do what he wants to do.

'As for Lineker, he is a sweet goalscorer.'

Lineker is third top goalscorer for England, but he is still behind Jimmy Greaves, for club and country! What's more Spurs have been blessed with exceptional strikers like Bobby Smith, Alan Gilzean, Steve Archibald, and Clive Allen, who scored 49 goals in one season.

Terry Venables was recently commissioned to produce a video of his Greatest Ever Tottenham Team, selecting his best player for each position. Neither Gascoigne, nor Lineker, both his own signings, made the star-studded team. He also felt that perhaps one day they will earn the distinction of joining the Tottenham Greats.

The fact that players of the calibre of Gascoigne and Lineker, plus numerous other top-class internationals, cannot make the Spurs side is proof, if ever it was needed, of the degree of difficulty, first in anyone selecting the best, and for those wanting the honour of selection.

I make no excuses for relying heavily on Bill Nicholson's undisputed expertise in reaching my conclusions.

I had the honour of assisting Bill Nick with his best-selling autobiography *Glory, Glory — My Life With Spurs*, published in 1984.

I spent many a happy and busy time at Bill's home — still only a football kick from the White Hart Lane ground — talking endlessly about his marvellous time at Spurs, 16 years as the club's most successful manager, and many more years as player and coach. He still works for the club he has served for more than half a century.

I asked Bill: 'Pick your best ever side for a chapter for the book.' He was most reluctant to agree. Eventually, after a great deal of thought, he capitulated, and he wrote: 'I have always been reluctant to join in the debate because it is such an impossible choice. Not only have there been some remarkable footballers over the years at White Hart Lane, but the game has also changed fundamentally in that time.

'I have always avoided picking my best XI before, and I am not going to commit myself now. But I will name a pool of players who would probably win the Championship or one of the Cup Finals if they were all available for the club next season.

'There is no foolproof means of assessing one style of play against another. Who is to say whether it is harder to play today than it was in the '50s? In my playing days pitches were far worse, the ball was heavier and it was a physically harder game. It took six months just to break a pair of football boots in! But there were players in those days who would be just as outstanding in today's conditions . . .'

I make no excuses for following Bill Nicholson's lead and adhering to his choice. I wonder where he would now place young Gazza . . .

CHAPTER 2

Dave Mackay

DAVE MACKAY HOLDS THE DISTINCTION OF being nominated by Bill Nicholson as his greatest ever signing — and that's some achievement.

Nicholson signed players of the calibre of Jimmy Greaves, Pat Jennings, Cliff Jones, John White, Mike England, Alan Mullery, Alan Gilzean, Cyril Knowles, Martin Chivers, Martin Peters and Bobby Smith as well as Mackay.

Nicholson says: 'I suppose most people would assume my choice would be Greaves because he was the best striker of his era and the game is about scoring goals. Greaves had a far superior goal record to any of his foremost contemporaries, including Denis Law, George Best, and Bobby Charlton. It is very hard to choose from among half a dozen of my players, but I think I must select Dave Mackay as my best-ever signing.

'Not only did Mackay make such an enormous contribution on the field but his dynamic character was also a major influence in training, and everywhere he went and in everything he did. The effect on other players was remarkable.

'He was truly a great player with far more skill than he was ever given credit for. He had a delicate touch, two good feet and was such an intelligent reader of the game that it came as no surprise to me that Brian Clough converted him into a sweeper at Derby.

'In midfield for Tottenham, Mackay was a mighty player, powerful in the tackle and very fair.'

Mackay was a true hard man. An immortal picture by my

one-time *Daily Mirror* colleague Monte Fresco captured Mackay, who felt he was the victim of an unfair tackle, grabbing Billy Bremner by the scruff of his shirt, snarling menacingly, as he held him up two foot off the ground. Bremner, with the reputation of the hardman of his era, shrugged his shoulders and looked apologetically and innocently at Mackay.

Mackay, his courage unquestioned after his fightback from a twice broken leg, would put the hard boys of today like Vinny Jones in the shade. Mackay was one of the most gifted individuals in addition to being a tough but scrupulously fair player who inspired his team-mates and led by example.

Alan Mullery was another with a heart of a lion. Again hard, but fair. He recalls the excessive training under Nicholson and the scraps between players with an iron will to win, none more so than Mackay. Mullery says: 'I remember the first day Terry Venables had at the club. In the very first minute of the five-a-side he stuck his backside out and knocked Dave Mackay over. Dave got up and kicked him up the backside and it led to a right old scrap.'

Nicholson signed Mackay from Hearts on 17 March 1959 for £32,000 just a few hours before the transfer deadline . . . in today's inflated transfer market Mackay would be the first £3 million player and set a new British record transfer.

Nicholson recalls: 'I will always remember the first day he arrived at our training ground after I bought him. The other players were shaken by his commitment and drive. They looked at each other as if to say, "What's happening here?" At the time he had a collection of seasoned professionals, most of them internationals, and Mackay was able to stir them all up. He brought a new surge into every aspect of club life, particularly in training.

'Suddenly our training routines became just as important as the matches. Mackay was a bit of a show-off when it came to the skills of the game and was also a brilliant tactician. Six-a-side games and full-scale practice matches assumed a greater

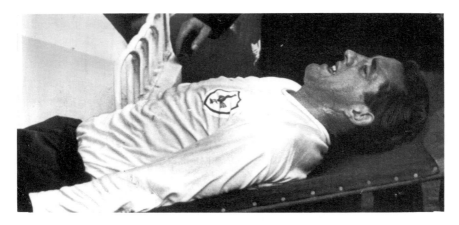

Dave Mackay's comeback bid ends in agony and heartbreak. After suffering a double fracture, the lion-hearted Mackay breaks the same leg on exactly the same spot after just 20 minutes in front of just 3,500 people in a reserve game at White Hart Lane.

importance. He had to be a winner. His barrel chest would be thrust out and he would emerge on the winning side, no matter what the odds against him. If he had served in a war, he would have been the first man into action. He would have won the Victoria Cross.'

Mackay is Terry Venables' hero. Venables admires the perfect blend of talent and guts. Venables paid £2 million to bring Paul Gascoigne to White Hart Lane. Venables has perceived signs of Mackay in young Gazza. For a start there are similarities in appearance, with Gazza's barrel chest. But if Gazza ever needed reminding how to tackle, hard but fair, and how to dominate the midfield, then he need only listen to Venables, or indeed Nicholson detail the technique of Mackay.

Venables says: 'Dave Mackay, for me, is one of the most charismatic footballers of all time. One of the best characters I've ever known in the game.

'He was a truly great player, and everyone talked about him as a rugged, tough midfield player, yet he was definitely one of the best one-touch players I've seen.

'There are some great stories about Dave. He would throw the opposition the ball when he ran on the field. "Here it is", he would say, "have a kick now because you won't get one when the game starts".

'We used to play in the gym. Eddie Bailey was the coach. He would give us a ball each, and there would be coloured lines on the wall, red, yellow and blue. Eddie Bailey would say — I'm sure he just made it up as he went along — chip the ball against the blue line, catch it on your thigh, bounce it up onto the red line, volley it against the yellow line, bounce it down on your chest, then your head, volley against the white line, and as it comes down "kill" it dead.

'We would all look at each other and think "terrific, Eddie!" Who could possibly understand it, let alone do it? Dave would say "hold on a minute", and chip, thigh, volley, back on his chest, head, volley back against the white line and kill it stone dead . . . "do you mean that, Eddie?" '

Nicholson says: 'Mackay brought many players tumbling to the ground with the ferocity of his tackling, but was scrupulously fair, always going for the ball.'

Nicholson was not surprised by the way Mackay grabbed hold of Bremner after the Leeds captain's tackle on the Spurs player. 'From what is generally known of Bremner, it could be said that he probably asked for it.

'Dave Mackay had a strict code of conduct. He tackled robustly but always fairly, and expected similar treatment himself. But if anyone went outside the rules he became very angry indeed, and the Bremner incident was one of those occasions.'

It illustrated the degree of class at the time that Nicholson can find an even greater, more inspirational skipper than Mackay. It seems inconceivable . . . until Nicholson mentions the name of Danny Blanchflower.

'Mackay would have been my first choice as captain, except that we already had a great one in Danny Blanchflower.

'Mackay was a carefree type of person, the opposite to Blanchflower. But they had a great respect for each other.

They were one of the outstanding partnerships of British football.

'When Blanchflower retired, Mackay took over for a while. He inspired and stimulated the team. There was no doubt we had a first-rate team before he arrived, but he seemed to provide an extra spark and give added momentum. I knew we needed to make a new signing as we entered into the sixties. Mackay probably did more than anyone to forge a team capable of winning the Double.' Naturally, for that reason Nicholson had no hesitation in choosing Mackay as his most important and his best-ever signing.

For that reason, the acquisition of Mackay, a vital ingredient to bring the Double to White Hart Lane, is one of the more important transfer stories in Spurs history.

Incredibly, Nicholson almost signed Mel Charles, brother of John Charles, instead!

Nicholson first became aware of Mackay's potential when he was put in charge of the England under-23 team by England manager Walter Winterbottom. At that time Nicholson was assistant manager and coach to Jimmy Anderson at Spurs.

As soon as Nicholson was appointed manager, Mackay was one of the names he put down on his list of potential signings, but when he inquired Hearts boss Tommy Walker said that Mackay was 'not available'.

But Swansea were ready to sell Mel Charles and Nicholson travelled to South Wales to interview him. 'I was not excited about Charles. His best position was centre half and we already had Maurice Norman. He could also play in other positions, notably centre forward where we were well served by Bobby Smith. When I spoke to him I hoped he would tell me he would like to play in other positions but he didn't do so. He indicated that he would give me his answer by Saturday night.

'He duly rang on time and said: "Sorry, Mr Nicholson, but I've decided to join Arsenal." I was relieved. "Okay son," I said. "Thanks for ringing and I wish you all the best of luck with Arsenal." Mel wasn't too successful and eventually returned home to Wales.'

Nicholson was soon back on the phone to Tommy Walker in Edinburgh. The transfer deadline was on Monday and Nicholson pushed hard. The two finally agreed a fee and Nicholson asked Walker to make sure that Mackay wanted to join Spurs before he made the trip to Scotland.

Once Mackay said 'yes', Nicholson caught the night train, arriving in Walker's office early next morning. A few hours before the midnight deadline the deal was sealed and Spurs were on their way to winning the Double.

As Walker took Nicholson to the station after lunch, the stationmaster, splendid in top hat, spotted the Hearts manager who introduced Nicholson to him.

'The stationmaster asked why I was there. "Hearts have just sold Dave Mackay to us." He was shocked,' recalls Nicholson.

Mackay was the heart and soul of the Spurs Double side. 'He tackled like a clap of thunder,' fellow Scot Tommy Docherty once said.

Mackay first broke his leg in a European Cup Winners Cup tie against Manchester United at Old Trafford on 11 December 1963.

The game was eight minutes old when Mackay went into a 50-50 tackle with Noel Cantwell, United's Irish defender. His leg was shattered in two places.

Mackay was in plaster for 16 weeks. When he started exercises once the plaster was removed his left leg was four inches thinner than his right leg!

Mackay was determination personified in his efforts to fight his way back to fitness. Nicholson knew the torture he was putting himself through. 'He sat for hours every day lifting a 15lb weight on his foot to strengthen it. No one has ever worked harder to get back to fitness. Tottenham lost 4-1 that night at Old Trafford, but such was Mackay's influence on the side at the time that I was convinced we would not have lost had he not been injured.'

Nearly a year later, Mackay made his comeback. On 12

Terry Venables watches one of the most famous scenes in soccer — the bust up between Scots Mackay and Bremner at White Hart Lane on 22nd August, 1966.

September 1964, he played against Shrewsbury reserves. Again, he was hurt in a tackle with Peter Colby and X-rays revealed a fracture to the same leg.

Nicholson says: 'Apparently the bones had joined together too solidly the first time, affecting his blood circulation. I was with the first team at West Ham when I heard the distressing news. I returned to White Hart Lane and was told Dave had said, "Bill Nick is going to go mad when he hears about this".

'I drove to the hospital. "Well, Dave," I said, "you've done it again". He smiled, and told him: "There are lessons to be learned from the first time, aren't there?" I was referring to the fact that he allowed his weight to increase while inactive, making it difficult to regain fitness when he resumed training. The extra weight put a burden on his left leg.

'This time he was careful not to eat or drink so much. I never knew anyone so determined to get back onto a football field. It was being suggested that he might never play again and that spurred him on. The two breaks left him with a slightly misshapen leg, but it didn't worry him or restrict his movements.'

Mackay won three F.A. Cup winners medals with Spurs before he was sold to Derby County in 1968 for £5,000.

The greatly reduced fee was a reward for Mackay's loyalty, status, and contribution to the club.

Clough moved Mackay back to play alongside the centre half. It worked so well that Mackay was voted Footballer of the Year by the Football Writers Association jointly with Manchester City's Tony Book.

He completed his distinguished playing career at Swindon, where he moved into management, before switching to boss of Nottingham Forest. Mackay made a huge impact in management when he led Derby to the League Championship in 1975 after the bitter and controversial departure of Brian Clough. He returned to the Baseball Ground after Clough's sensational resignation in 1973 to join Leeds — which lasted just 44 days. Mackay was greeted by a players' rebellion. They wanted Clough back. They even threatened strike action. There were 4,000 Clough supporters meeting every Saturday plotting Clough's return. Mackay stayed silent until he heard that Mrs Clough planned to lead the wives on a protest march through the town. Mackay clenched his fists, brought the players into his room individually and some straight talking ended a ludicrous situation with handshakes all round. The nonsense ended, Derby finished third and won the title the next year.

In 1976, the year after winning the title at Derby, he probably would have survived a boardroom coup had he not insisted on a vote of confidence from them.

'I knew they weren't going to back me but I'm a funny lad. I just didn't want to work in an atmosphere which wasn't enjoyable. There was a faction there who wanted Brian Clough back and moaned about anything I did. Even though we finished third, first and fourth when I was there. When I

Manchester United right winger Albert Quixall makes a gesture of apology to Mackay after pulling the Spurs player down in a tackle during the match at Old Trafford. Mackay brushed him aside, not the least bit interested in his apology.

bought Francis Lee they said he was past it. When I bought Charlie George they said he was a tearaway. If I had bought Maradona they would have said he had no right foot. I'd had enough of it.'

Next step along his amazing management route was Walsall, where he kept an almost doomed side up and the next season he almost took them to promotion. Walsall were third from the bottom with 15 games left. Mackay took Walsall on a run of nine games unbeaten.

Mackay was enticed to the Middle East on a lucrative contract. There he won five League titles with Al Arabi, and won once in four finals in the Gulf Cup.

He spent nine years in the desert, eight in Kuwait and one in Dubai, only to come home to discover English football was a desert, lacking in real characters and class. That's why Mackay wants to see young Paul Gascoigne thrive. In December '88 I interviewed Mackay for the *Daily Mirror* on the subject of Gazza. He told me: 'I'm pleased they're comparing this young lad with me, because the game desperately and urgently needs this type of player. I've been so saddened by the defensive nature of our game now. When I left for the Middle East it was defensive enough, but when I came back it was even more so. It means there are a lot of boring games. In my days there were five forwards. The last time Spurs had any success they used just one, Clive Allen. I like good footballing teams like West Ham, Spurs, Manchester United, Everton and Liverpool. But it seems that Liverpool are the only club over the last 20 years who have consistently managed to combine entertaining and successful football. As for players I'd go out of my way to watch, I suppose there's Ian Rush and now Gascoigne. But he's still got to prove himself. He made a bad start but he has overcome that, so that's a good sign. I know he loves clowning in a game, but football has become so serious, certainly far more serious than it used to be. Twenty years ago, the spectator would accept a 4-3 defeat, but they won't accept it now. Results are all that counts. That only puts more pressure on the modern-day player. Great players inspire me and I'd love to see someone like Gascoigne succeeding. But it won't be easy.'

Mackay returned to English football as manager of Doncaster. 'When I first came back I promised myself a year off. I'd been away nine years, earned a few quid and I felt I wouldn't mind putting my feet up. But after a couple of months I got bored. I had to do something and the only things

Mackay takes the lucrative and successful road to Middle East football.

I'd ever done for a living were — one, be a joiner, which I don't like, and two, be in football, which I did.'

Again he showed his dogged character when he quit after a row with his directors when he was ordered to sell the best of his young players. He walked out on Doncaster in March 1989 and made his comeback the following month as boss of Birmingham City. In May '89, just a few weeks after the horrors of Hillsborough when 95 fans lost their lives, Birmingham fans were involved in pitched battles at Crystal Palace. Mounted riot police charged in to break up the mindless violence and 20 minutes after the stoppage Mackay went to the large contingent of travelling Birmingham fans and appealed to them to behave. He said: 'The only way we can save this game is for you to behave. The players want to play. Please give me a chance.' Mackay added later: 'It was just a bit worrying to say the least. I'm just glad it's over. We brought too many people. But at least the fences were down so people could reach the pitch. The police did a good job.'

Mackay is just as tough as a manager as he ever was as a player.

DAVE MACKAY'S PLAYING CAREER

	LEAGUE		F.A. CUP		F.L. CUP		EUROPE		TOTAL	
	App	Gls	App	Gls	App	Gls	App	Gls	App	Gls
1958-59	4								4	
1959-60	38	11	3						41	11
1960-61	37	4	7	2					44	6
1961-62	26	8	7				7	2	40	10
1962-63	37	6	1				6	2	44	8
1963-64	17	3					2	1	19	4
1964-65	NO APPEARANCES									
1965-66	41	6	2	2					43	8
1966-67	39	3	8						47	3
1967-68	29	1	5				2		36	3
	268	42	33	4			17	5	318	53

SCOTLAND: 1959 v England, West Germany, Northern Ireland, Wales; 1960 v Poland, Austria, Hungary, Turkey, Wales, Northern Ireland; 1961 v England; 1963 v England, Australia, Norway, Northern Ireland, Norway, Wales; 1965 v Northern Ireland (18 caps).

CHAPTER 3

Ronnie Burgess

'**H**E RESEMBLED BRYAN ROBSON. NO, HE WAS better than the England and Manchester United captain.'

That's the astonishing assessment of Ronnie Burgess by Bill Nicholson. That is the reason Nicholson would write the name Burgess first in any team sheet he would select.

Tottenham's manager from their glory, glory days, Bill Nicholson, and current boss Terry Venables have one thing in common when it came to selecting their greatest ever Tottenham team. They both chose Ronnie Burgess.

That is a powerful argument for including a player in my selection even although I have never seen him play. Who am I to argue with Nicholson and Venables?

In fact, I have a suspicion that when Venables made his selection for a Christmas video he leaned heavily on the advice of Bill Nick. No man is better qualified to make a judgement on Tottenham players than Bill Nicholson.

In his autobiography *Glory, Glory — My Life with Spurs*, Nicholson explained to me exactly why such a task of selecting his greatest ever Spurs stars was too difficult.

'There is no foolproof means of assessing one style of play against another. Who is to say whether it is harder to play today than it was in the '50s? In my playing days pitches were far worse, the ball was heavier and it was a physically harder game. It took six months just to break a pair of boots in! But there were players in those days who would be just as outstanding in today's conditions and the first one who comes to mind is Ronnie Burgess, who was a groundstaff colleague when I first joined the club. Ron is the first player I would select in the 'best ever' Tottenham side. He had all the requirements of the perfect footballer. He was well-built at just under six feet in height, with tremendous stamina, speed and agility and had great control and mastery of the ball. He was also a magnificent tackler, a good header of the ball and a brilliant passer. He could strike the ball equally well with either foot and was a sound positional player.'

Burgess, a Welsh wing-half, joined Spurs at the same time as Nicholson, who earned the royal salary of £2-a-week! Burgess became captain of the club after the war.

Nicholson recalls: 'I liked him very much. He was genuine and honest and, although he later became captain, he was never afraid to seek advice. There were times when he sought it too often. Before he tossed up, he would say: 'Which way should we kick?'

'But that is not to belittle him; in those days the best player usually became the captain whatever his leadership qualities. Ron was too nice a person to order people about and make decisions affecting their livelihoods which was the main reason he was less successful as a manager than he had been as a player.

'He was my favourite player in my years at Tottenham. He had everything: good feet, ability in the air, strength in the tackle and was a beautiful passer of the ball. In some ways he resembled Bryan Robson, the Manchester United and England captain. But I believe he was a better player than Bryan Robson.

'Ron and I spent our first two years painting the grandstand and working on the pitch. I dreaded having to paint the girders of the stands because I had no head for heights. Not much of our time was occupied in playing football. Training for the groundstaff lads was confined to Tuesday and Thursday afternoons, but when we had a spare moment we would kick about under the stands using a bundle of old cloth tied up into a ball.'

Ron Burgess is rated as better than Bryan Robson by his one-time team-mate Bill Nicholson. Burgess is pictured at the start of the 1950 season.

Nicholson and Burgess were team-mates in an exhilarating '50s team under manager Arthur Rowe, his tactics dubbed 'push and run'.

Such was the magic of the attacking, entertaining football that the average attendance was 54,405, a figure that will never be beaten by any First Division club, unless they build a new stadium bigger than any of the current First Division grounds in this country.

Spurs would dominate their home matches with so much attacking football that centre half Harry Clarke would always be moaning. Nicholson recalls: 'He used to sit next to me in the dressing room afterwards and I would say, "What's up Harry?"

"I only touched the ball nine times," he would reply. "I didn't get a kick or a header. You're mopping everything up on one side and Ron Burgess on the other. I'm left doing nothing."

The team possessed class performers, wingers Sonny Walters and Les Medley with Eddie Bailey, rated the best first-time passer of the ball Nicholson has ever seen. There was Alf Ramsey at full back, later to be knighted after winning the World Cup for England in 1966.

The days of the push and run were over when the influence of Arthur Rowe went into decline. His health suffered trying to avoid relegation, and Burgess departed for Swansea in 1954-5, and according to Nicholson 'his influence was sadly missed.'

But the name of Burgess lives on. He has stood the test of time as one of Tottenham's greatest players.

Terry Venables has seen numerous outstanding midfield players at Spurs. In fact he was one himself, although not readily accepted or appreciated by the Spurs fans at the time. John White, Tommy Harmer, Martin Peters, Eddie Bailey, Alan Mullery, and Ricky Villa would all qualify for most club's greatest ever midfield stars without any debate . . . but not so at Spurs.

It is a measure of the extensive amount of talent that has passed through the club over the years that there simply isn't room for them all. It is with great sadness that the outstanding John White is just edged out. Venables says: 'I actually played against him, and I found him one of the most difficult players to play against. He was excellent. He was always on the move, knocking the ball off simply, not always appreciated by the crowd, because, quite naturally, they like to see clever things, but he played the game so simply. It was such a tragedy that he

Ron Burgess captained Spurs after the War and had a touch of Duncan Edwards about him, according to Terry Venables.

was killed by lightning. We never really knew how good this man was going to be . . . terrible shame.'

Then, there's Alan Mullery, another firm favourite of Venables. 'He was a great boisterous personality, a very solid character, a very honest footballer, a strong powerful man yet never dirty. He could do everything, running, tackling, shooting, short passing, powerful.'

Martin Peters scored for England in the World Cup Finals and came to Spurs in part exchange for Jimmy Greaves. 'Perhaps his best years were at West Ham. They called him the Duke because he looked like the Duke of Kent. He was an outstanding midfield talent, one of the best I've ever seen.' He was the player Sir Alf Ramsey dubbed "10 years ahead of his time". Venables explained. 'You couldn't coach into a player his timing to arrive on the scene.'

Tommy Harmer, 'Harmer the Charmer', was yet another exceptionally gifted midfield player, along with Johnny Brookes. Venables says: 'Tommy Harmer was a pint-sized magician. Even though you always thought he was a bit lightweight he was nonetheless a great player. Johnny Brookes was another great favourite of mine. He won three caps against Yugoslavia, Wales and Denmark and I thought he was unlucky not to win any more. I was a Johnny Brookes fan.'

Steve Perryman played his best football for Spurs in midfield and who can forget that Cup Final goal by Ricky Villa? The brilliant Argentinian weaved his way past the Manchester City defence to score one of the most spectacular goals Wembley has ever seen in an F.A. Cup Final.

When Venables consulted Nicholson, the name of Eddie Bailey was prominent. Venables says: 'Eddie Bailey was the best one-touch player Bill has ever seen. Bill was adamant that no-one could ever tackle Eddie because he was always gone by them before they had a chance. The Brazilians are universally praised for the sort of illusions they can conjure on a football field. They have plenty of tricks up their sleeves with one-touch football, but Bill says that Eddie was the best at that.'

With such a wealth and diversity of talent it would seem a midfield selection is virtually impossible. Personally I have selected Dave Mackay, Danny Blanchflower, Glenn Hoddle, and Burgess.

Burgess wins the Bill Nicholson vote and that is good enough for Venables, who says: 'Bill Nicholson says he is the best midfield player there has been at this club, and that's good enough for me.

'Bill says you could play him at the back, play him in midfield, play him at centre forward and he would be perfectly at home.

'You hear about soccer legends like Duncan Edwards who are able to play anywhere and Bill insists that Ronnie Burgess is like that. In that situation, of course, Burgess has got to be in the reckoning.'

Venables has been boyhood fan, player and manager; few are in a better position to judge but even he has to admit: 'It is well nigh impossible to pick the players, especially to satisfy everyone, because there are so many great players that go back such a long way.

'I saw my first game of football here at White Hart Lane when I was still at school. Then, I was able to get a pass and sit in front near where the players came out, I was so close I could almost touch them from where I sat, it was quite fantastic. The club has had its highs and lows, but when it has not been winning things they have played a quality brand of football — they have always played quality football.'

Ronnie Burgess has been one of those players of the highest quality, if not *the* highest.

RONNIE BURGESS' PLAYING CAREER

	LEAGUE		F.A. CUP		F.L. CUP		EUROPE		TOTAL	
	App	Gls	App	Gls	App	Gls	App	Gls	App	Gls
1938-39	17	1							17	1
1946-47	40	5	2						42	5
1947-48	32	2	4						36	2
1948-49	41	3	1						42	3
1949-50	39		3						42	
1950-51	35	2	1						36	2
1951-52	40		2						42	
1952-53	30	2	7						37	2
1953-54	24		5						29	
	298	15	25						323	15

WALES: 1946 v Scotland, England; 1947 v Northern Ireland, England, Scotland; 1948 v Scotland, England; 1949 v Northern Ireland, Portugal, Belgium, Switzerland, England, Scotland, Belgium; 1950 v Northern Ireland, Scotland; 1951 v Northern Ireland, Portugal, Switzerland, England, Scotland, Rest of United Kingdom; 1952 v Northern Ireland, Scotland, England; 1953 v Northern Ireland, France, Yugoslavia, England, Scotland; 1954 v Northern Ireland, Austria (22 caps).

CHAPTER 4

Danny Blanchflower

DANNY BLANCHFLOWER LIVES IN THE MEMORY as one of the most immaculate footballers ever, not only in the context of his illustrious career with Spurs, but in British football.

After quitting as a player Blanchflower wrote a most readable and intelligent column in Fleet Street. He didn't need to have it 'ghost written', he actually penned it himself! He could talk for hours, endlessly discussing the virtues of the game, the aspects of football that are so precious to him — skill and honesty. Regrettably, he now keeps himself to himself, a virtual recluse, not even playing his beloved golf too much these days.

But Blanchflower will forever be upheld in the football community as a player of quite exceptional talent, an outstanding captain and leader of men, and a perceptive football brain.

Terry Venables says: 'I always got the feeling that when Danny Blanchflower played, he had it all worked out, like a professor playing football. The weight of his passing was perfection. Somehow he didn't quite look as though he should have been a footballer, he was out of some different world, like an aristocrat from a Squire Magazine, and he played like that . . . a very bright, intelligent man who went on to be a very fine sports journalist.'

Bill Nicholson has fond memories of him . . .

'Danny was my first captain when I became manager. He was a player who knew his own mind. He thought a lot of himself and I thought a lot of him. He had imagination. He perceived what was happening in a game and provided answers. Even when I dropped him from the team, he was able to sit down and calmly assess the reasons.

'He was an extremely able captain because he could communicate so well. He would come into my office and we would sit down and discuss things in depth. We would talk over players and he would advise me about their mood. He might say that certain ideas of mine might not be well received. He was my listening-post.

'Danny was full of talk. Towards the end of his playing days I asked him to become my assistant and help me with training. He agreed, but soon found his position within the first-team group of players was no longer the _same. Conversation tailed away when he came into the dressing rooms or showers. "That's because they look on you as one of the governors," I told him.'

Blanchflower should have actually become the governor of the team as Nicholson wanted him to succeed him as manager, even though after he retired as a player he had switched very successfully to TV and newspapers, although he did manage the Northern Ireland team, demonstrating his usual positive approach irrespective of results.

It is one of my biggest regrets that Danny Blanchflower never succeeded Bill Nicholson as Tottenham Hotspur manager. The opportunity to establish a Spurs dynasty on the Liverpool lines had been lost forever.

Nicholson had thought, after he resigned as Spurs boss, that the directors had asked him to stay on to help choose his successor. He was so convinced of his mandate that he set about the task of linking Danny Blanchflower with Johnny Giles as the No. 2. He interviewed them both, and they wanted the job. It was a huge shock to Nicholson that the Spurs chairman Sidney Wale opted to ignore his professional advice and chose Terry Neill instead.

As the 'Spurs Reporter' on the local *Tottenham Weekly Herald* newspaper, with the main building 200 yards from the

Danny Blanchflower with Tommy Docherty, the then Chelsea manager, as guests of honour at the Variety Club of Great Britain's opening luncheon in 1963 at the Savoy Hotel.

White Hart Lane ground, I would often wander into the club's offices as part of my reporting duties.

Shortly after Nicholson's shock resignation I walked into the office and bumped into Danny Blanchflower. He was waiting to see Nicholson. It didn't take a genius to work out what was afoot. Blanchflower confided in me that he was being interviewed for the post as Spurs manager — or at least he and Bill Nicholson thought that was the case. He asked me to keep his appointment confidential and in return he would give me a full interview should he be accepted as the Spurs manager.

I thought, at the time, and have no reason to change my opinion, that Blanchflower was a natural for the job, and had he got it would have begun the same line of succession to the management throne at Spurs that Bill Shankly established within Anfield.

In the enjoyable course of recording Bill Nicholson's

A game of pool for Northern Ireland manager Danny Blanchflower and his players, including Pat Jennings, at the Esso Hotel in Coventry.

autobiography, he confided: 'I naturally assumed I would be allowed to nominate my successor as manager of the club. After all, I had virtually run Tottenham for sixteen years. The directors had a comparatively easy time in those years, enjoying the matches and the glory and leaving me to take the strain. At Liverpool, the best-run club in Britain, Bill Shankly had attended the meeting of the directors which decided to appoint Bob Paisley to succeed him. And I have no doubt that Bob Paisley's recommendation about his own successor was heeded by the Liverpool directors and that led to the promotion of Joe Fagan to the number one job at Anfield.

'I did not know the Tottenham board had anyone in mind as the new manager. They did not confide in me. My guess is that they had no idea. The man I wanted was Danny Blanchflower. Even though he had been out of the game for some time, apart from writing a weekly column in the *Sunday Express*, it was my opinion that he would still have made an exceptional manager for the club. He kept in close contact with people in the game, including me, and I thought he was the outstanding candidate. He had similar ideas to mine about

The 'Double' team reunion in London 28 years on with captain Danny Blanchflower, and manager Bill Nicholson from the 1961 era flanking goalkeeper Ted Ditchburn.

how the game should be played. He knew the Tottenham set up and its tradition. And he was popular and a man with a sense of humour.

'I interviewed Danny for the job of manager of Tottenham. He knew his relationship with the players would be different and he accepted that. Typically he wanted to know all the details. He was very interested and after a long talk, decided he'd like the job. He said he wanted me to stay on in the background and I was prepared to do that. Bob Paisley's advice is still available at Anfield and I believe that it is important to have experienced managers to call upon.

'I intended to be a general advisor to Danny when he took over. I would not have permitted players to seek advice from me behind his back. It would have been the ideal working relationship. Although different in personality, we shared the same ideals.

'There was another person I thought might make a good

Danny Blanchflower and Sir Stanley Matthews pick up yet more awards for their services to soccer. This time it's the Whitebread British Sports Awards in March 1983.

manager of Tottenham — Johnny Giles, captain of Leeds and Ireland. I rang him and asked him to travel down to be interviewed and he agreed. I spent an entire afternoon with him and was most impressed. He had all the requirements and I thought he would make a good manager. Even Danny approved. Had Danny been appointed manager, he would have wanted Johnny as his player-coach. Giles had had experience of management with Ireland and had learned from his years working under Don Revie at Elland Road. I was sure at the time that he was capable of making the jump from player to manager.

'I felt confident that I had done my best to ensure that the running of the club would remain in good hands. During my second week as temporary manager — the two weeks' extra time I had agreed to serve — a board meeting was called at the club to discuss the applications for a new manager. To my great surprise I was not called to the meeting. I really couldn't believe this because I had previously told the Chairman that I

Danny Blanchflower won 56 Northern Ireland caps and captained his country to some notable successes.

had interviewed Blanchflower and Giles and would like to submit a report on both of them for consideration as my successor. I said that I felt they both had the right qualifications and had my full support.

'I was shocked by the response from the board, chairman Sidney Wale in particular. He was upset that I had interviewed the two men without his knowledge or approval. The other directors appeared to share his indignation.

'I was angry too because they had asked me to continue as manager and all the time I had been in charge they had never

Danny Blanchflower exhibits the measured style in training on the day the European Cup Winners' Cup was on show at the club's former training headquarters at Cheshunt.

Coach, manager, player, newspaper columnist — Danny Blanchflower had it all until he blew the whistle on his involvement in the game.

queried any of my decisions. They knew my motives were sound. Everything I undertook was for the good of the club. No one worked harder or longer than me in its interests. I told them in no uncertain manner that what I had done was for the benefit of Tottenham. I was using the experience of my lifetime in the game to find a man capable of taking over a great club. I

Danny Blanchflower should have succeeded Bill Nicholson as Spurs manager . . . but he eventually had only a brief flirtation as boss of Chelsea.

felt the directors must be interested in what I had to say. Instead, my recommendations were ignored.

'I believed I was doing Danny Blanchflower and Johnny Giles a service by interviewing them, but as it turned out I was doing them a disservice. I had killed off any chance they had of being short-listed for the post.

'Why the Chairman should have such strong objections I really do not know. I felt the directors were making excuses. Had Blanchflower taken over, there would have been a new look to the team and possibly even to the running of the club. Perhaps they felt their position had been threatened in some way.'

Nicholson had tried to buy Mick Lyons from Everton, opened talks on a swap deal with Martin Chivers exchanged for Stan Bowles while QPR manager Gordon Jago gave the outgoing Spurs manager the impression Gerry Francis and Don Givens could be bought. Nicholson even consulted Blanchflower, and the new-look team had 'excited' him. He also wanted Giles in his midfield. But the board ignored Nicholson and a couple of days later appointed Terry Neill, and the Nicholson era was over.

Blanchflower began his Spurs career as a replacement for Nicholson. The articulate Irishman was in dispute with Aston Villa, and although he was 29, his club wanted £40,000, a grand sum at that time for someone of his age, and £6,000 more than the then record fee paid by Sheffield Wednesday to Notts County for Jackie Sewell.

Nicholson recalls: 'Arsenal were the first club to bid but Tom Whittaker, their manager, failed to persuade his directors to increase their offer beyond £28,500.' After several weeks Villa accepted Spurs' bid of £30,000. Danny was staying in a London hotel with the Northern Ireland team when the deal was concluded. Nicholson goes on: 'There was a phone call for a Mr Blanchflower and a voice said: 'Eric here, you've been transferred to Spurs.' The call was taken by Jackie Blanchflower, Danny's brother who was also in the Irish team. Eric was Eric Houghton, the Villa manager.'

Spurs quickly discovered that they had bought a far from ordinary footballer.

Nicholson takes up the story again: 'He had written a weekly column in the *Birmingham Argus* and had agreed to write a similar column for a Fleet Street newspaper. The FA reminded the club that players were forbidden to write in newspapers. The directors asked him to stop but he refused. Eventually a compromise was worked out whereby we agreed to have his articles vetted, but as far as I know no one at the club ever saw them before they went into print. Danny was a good writer. He had a feel for words and a love of the game.'

Spurs were knocked out of the F.A. Cup 3-1 at Bootham Crescent, and not long afterwards Arthur Rowe fell ill and resigned. Jimmy Anderson, the man in plus-fours, replaced Rowe and one of his first acts was to drop Alf Ramsey and install Blanchflower as club captain. Nicholson says: 'He took an increasingly important role in the team. He didn't see his role as captain merely to toss up and decide which way to kick. He considered it gave him the authority to change the side if things were going badly and he made a decisive switch in the sixth round of the F.A. Cup against West Ham when his team were losing 3-1 with 20 minutes to go. He ordered Maurice Norman up into the attack and Tottenham earned a replay which they won 2-1. The directors didn't complain that time because the move worked but when Blanchflower tried it again in the semi-final against Manchester City at Villa Park and the gamble failed, City winning a dull match 1-0, they were livid.' The Cup defeat that season left the club battling against relegation. Over Easter the team lost at home to Huddersfield 2-1, and again Blanchflower ordered a defender into attack. Anderson was furious and stormed into the dressing rooms to vent his feelings on Blanchflower.

Blanchflower paid for using his initiative with the axe, and Harry Clarke, a reluctant leader, was handed the captaincy. Blanchflower was still out of favour the following season, 1956-57, when the club scored more goals, 104, than any other First Division side and finished second behind Manchester United.

Still denied the captaincy, he had one of his best seasons in 1957-58 when Spurs finished third behind champions Wolves, and Blanchflower was voted Player of the Year by the Football Writers Association. 'A well deserved honour,' said Nicholson.

The next season was a disaster. Blanchflower and Harmer were dropped in turn, and Jimmy Anderson was replaced as manager by Nicholson before the Everton match. Spurs won 10-4 in Nicholson's first match in charge and Blanchflower said in the dressing rooms afterwards: 'It can only get worse!'

Typically of Nicholson, the new manager was not happy with the way the defence had conceded four goals. Nicholson says: 'The defence kept giving away silly goals and we spent most of the season in the bottom third of the table. I told Danny I thought he was one of the culprits. I said: ''You're taking too many liberties. When the ball is played into our box you're often on your way out looking for a throw from the keeper. You should be in that box marking someone and doing your defensive job.''

'After my prodding on this point, he became a better defensive player. I told him it was all very well being one of the outstanding attacking midfield players in the country but when the move broke down he became a defender along with the other players.'

Nicholson axed Blanchflower at the start of 1959, explaining he would be out for a few games. Spurs won those games and Blanchflower accepted the manager was right.

It prompted Blanchflower, at the age of 33, to ask for a transfer.

Nicholson rejected it. 'There was no acrimony. He was one player you could have a rational discussion with and still remain friends. I knew we needed his captaincy and in March I restored him to the job for a match against the eventual champions, Wolves, at Molineux which we drew 1-1.'

Spurs escaped relegation by six points, but the acquisition of first Cliff Jones and then Dave Mackay to partner Blanchflower in midfield, and the return of Tony Marchi from Italy, began the final touches to the eventual Double winning team of 1960-61. Nicholson also signed Bill Brown from Dundee for £16,500. Nicholson recalls: 'I felt we were building a side that could win a trophy.' Spurs almost won the title, finishing third behind Burnley. In October Nicholson signed John White from Falkirk for £20,000, and in December Les Allen arrived from Chelsea. Nicholson says: 'Danny Blanchflower claims that he told Fred Bearman, the Tottenham chairman at the start of the 1960-61 season: ''I am

Past and present Tottenham Greats Danny Blanchflower and Paul Gascoigne, before the testimonial at White Hart Lane.

sure we can do the Double this season.'' Danny is like all Irishmen, a romantic and a story teller, but I do know that I felt we had the makings of a good side. I felt we had a chance of the Double. I was optimistic.'

At the end of the season Danny Blanchflower climbed the

39 steps to the Royal Box to receive the F.A. Cup from the Duchess of Kent, to fulfill his prediction to Fred Bearman that the Double could be achieved.

Of course Arsenal and Liverpool have followed suit this Century . . . but the first is always the hardest. In fact no-one thought it could be done, but Blanchflower, to his eternal credit, did.

It was so sad to see Blanchflower's personal life decline in later life.

But his friends rallied round.

Billy Bingham contacted Spurs manager Terry Venables to organise a testimonial at White Hart Lane.

It was a touching moment when one of Tottenham's greatest players from the past met the new generation of superstar, Paul Gascoigne and the pair embraced before the start of the match, Spurs v Northern Ireland, with a number of guest players.

Gazza showed his cheek with a back flick from the penalty spot, a stunt that would have been admired by Blanchflower, a believer in the unorthodox.

Blanchflower has become disillusioned with the standard of football on these shores, but Gazza's performances in the World Cup would have lifted his spirits.

DANNY BLANCHFLOWER'S PLAYING CAREER

	LEAGUE		F.A. CUP		F.L. CUP		EUROPE		TOTAL	
	App	Gls	App	Gls	App	Gls	App	Gls	App	Gls
1954-55	22		3						25	
1955-56	40		6						46	
1956-57	39	1	3	1					42	2
1957-58	40		2						42	
1958-59	36	1	1						37	1
1959-60	40	2	4	1					44	3
1960-61	42	6	7				8	2	49	6
1961-62	39	2	7	2			4		54	6
1963-64	15								15	
	337	15	33	4			12	2	382	21

NORTHERN IRELAND: 1954 v England, Scotland; 1955 v Wales, Scotland, England; 1956 v Wales, England, Scotland; 1957 v Portugal, Wales, Italy, Portugal, Scotland, England, Italy; 1958 v Italy, Wales, Czechoslovakia, Argentina, West Germany, Czechoslovakia, France, England, Spain, Scotland; 1959 v Wales, Scotland, England; 1960 v Wales, England, West Germany, Scotland; 1961 v Wales, West Germany, Scotland, Greece, England; 1962 v Wales, Holland, Poland, England, Scotland, Poland (43 caps).

CHAPTER 5

Cliff Jones

FOR HIS SIZE CLIFF JONES WAS THE BEST HEADER of a ball I've ever seen. He would score spectacular goals with flying headers.

A return of 134 goals in 314 League games is an outstanding record for a winger.

His dribbling skills were something special. The players in the Double side would say that if ever they needed a rest they would simply give the ball to Jonesy.

Terry Venables stood on the Tottenham terraces as a boy, and Cliff Jones was one of his heroes.

Venables says: 'Of my time supporting Tottenham, and Bill Nick might agree, Cliff Jones was possibly the best winger the club had.

'I thought he was absolutely magnificent.'

The little Welsh wizard mesmerised defenders and enthralled the fans.

Venables recalls: 'Defenders would have to take a gamble when confronting him, they could bring him down or watch him go by them.

'His pace and change of direction made him such a tricky winger.

'He was not a big guy, yet he was able to get across defenders consistently with powerful headers.

'He must have had so many cuts on his face.'

Cliff Jones was a brave player, perhaps none braver. He is also a very nice, warm human being. A pleasure to talk to, always approachable and friendly. Still very much an enthusiast.

A sweat and sour goal for Cliff Jones . . . his last for Spurs in a match against Manchester United at White Hart Lane.

'When I was a cub reporter on the *North London Weekly Herald* newspaper, we had a five-a-side team that played at one of the local sports halls. I was playing for our works team in goal . . . against one of my boyhood heroes. Cliff Jones turned out for one of our opponents, and put four goals past me. After his career ended Cliff switched to local schools and sports complexes only too keen to pass on his knowledge to kids. As a games instructor he specialised in PE, football, swimming, and cricket at Highbury Grove School, Islington. 'Teaching is a Welsh industry, so it was right I should get involved.'

He originally invested all his savings in two butchers' shops in his heyday. But they went broke and for a time he was

None came braver or bolder than Cliff Jones. Spurs trainer Cecil Pointon helps Cliff off the field after a nasty gashed head in a collision during a match with Sheffield United.

on the breadline. For a while he was a porter in Covent Garden, then returned to his old trade as a sheet metalworker. At the time he said: 'Footballers thinking of investing in a career for the end of their playing days must be sure they know what they are doing, and spend as much time in the business as

Cliff Jones celebrates his recall to the Welsh side in 1966 with Lee Carmichael at the opening of a women's boutique in North London.

they can. They must always know what stock they have got and how much money is being paid into the bank. When I was down on my luck I took a six-month refresher course in my old sheet metal job.' But it's best to remember him for his tremendous ability and pleasure he gave to Spurs fans rather than his business failures.

Cliff Jones suffered his share of injuries. This time he's recovering at his Palmers Green house in 1966 from tearing a ligament in his ankle during training.

When 50,000 fans packed Molineux for the visit of Spurs, Jones was one of the goalscorers in a 4-0 win and he recalls the attitude of the Double side. 'We won things, we won the Double, but we went out to entertain as well. We expected to enjoy ourselves while we were playing. Now the players run out looking as if they are off to fight in Vietnam.'

Jones holds the distinction, along with Dave Mackay, of

taking part in the F.A. Cup Final triumphs of '61, '62, and '67. But Jones only won his third F.A. Cup winners' medal as the substitute in the '76 Final against Chelsea. After a series of injuries Jones had won back his place in the side. Then, in a League match against Leicester at White Hart Lane, he went up for a high ball with Derek Dougan . . . and finished on the ground with a dislocated shoulder. Although he fought back to fitness again, Frank Saul had grabbed his chance, kept his place in the side and justified his selection by scoring in the Final.

'I only got a kick before the match started, and things went so well during the game that I knew I would never get called on. Still in the end I did get my medal — it was the first year that the FA allowed 12 medals to be struck. But, of course, it wasn't the same. There's nothing that anybody can do to compensate for not playing in the match. I got the same medal, the same cash and the same perks as every other Spurs player . . . but it still wasn't the same.'

Jones picks out the 1962 Final against Burnley as his best. 'The game against Leicester was a bit disappointing, the quality of football wasn't up to what we'd expected. Leicester were down to 10 men after 35 minutes, and it put them back on the defensive. I'd say there was more atmosphere at the semi-final. Then there were the real supporters there — the Cup Final itself is too much of a glamour occasion. There's not enough in it for the genuine supporter. Even so, I'd rather play in a Cup Final than in any sort of match.'

Bill Nicholson recalls that Cliff Jones shared a fear of flying with Jimmy Greaves. 'Before departing on a European trip, the pair of them would slip away to the nearest bar for a quick drink to give them courage.'

He also remembers that Cliff Jones and Dave Mackay would share a laugh and a joke with John White, even though he was a shy and quiet member of the team at that time. They played a game with a half-crown piece. Nicholson recalls: 'They would flip it up from the foot to the forehead, catch it on their foot and flip it up again so that it landed in their pocket. They had competitions to see who could do it the most times. I don't see today's players doing anything like that.' At least that was the case until Paul Gascoigne came on the scene!

Nicholson paid a British record fee of £35,000 to Swansea for the Welsh winger, nephew of Bryan Jones. Cliff would be worth at least £2 million in today's transfer market. He would certainly be equal to, if not of greater value than, Chris Waddle, sold to Marseille for £4½ million.

But, unlike Bryan Jones when he joined Arsenal for a record fee before the war, Cliff Jones took some time to settle down at Spurs. Nicholson recalls: 'Despite his pace and ability to score, the crowd did not accept him for a time. He was helped by being out for a while with a hairline fracture. It gave him a more gradual introduction.

'Jimmy Anderson and I signed him when he was a private serving at a barracks in St. John's Wood. After being given permission by Swansea to talk to him, we arrived at the barracks to discover he was missing. No one knew his whereabouts and the suspicion was that he was absent without leave. 'We've got him into trouble,' said Jimmy Anderson. But things were sorted out the next day and he duly signed.

'Though he was a left-sided player who played the majority of his 318 League games on the left, Cliff was right-footed. I asked him why he played on the left and he said: 'The junior team I played for at home didn't have a left-winger so they put me there.' He seldom went on the outside of opponents. Invariably he would turn inside, and he had the Stan Matthews trick of being able to lift the ball over the stretched leg of an opponent. He got through more tackles that way than any player I knew. He was enormously brave and would go flying in at the far posts for headers like a centre forward. That first year he spent most of the time in the treatment room but the following season, 1958-59, he scored 20 goals from 38 games, a commendable record for a winger.'

If you want to get ahead, get a hat! Cliff Jones and Jimmy Greaves prove they took silly pictures in the 60's as well as now, as they celebrate at a party a win over great rivals Manchester United.

Nicholson had no doubt that during the Double season 'we had none braver than Jones and Mackay.'

In fact he says: 'There was no braver player in the game than Cliff, and for a small, slight man he scored some memorable goals with his head. All he needed was a few steps to obtain maximum height and he would soar over defenders. I told him: 'The defender cannot afford to make a mistake with his timing of the cross, while you can. Take a chance. 'I wanted him to make the most of every opportunity of trying to meet the ball ahead of his opponents. In the process he collected a few cuts around the eyes and head, but it never deterred him. He was indifferent to pain — like Bobby Smith.'

He went on to play for Fulham in 1968 for two years and also played for Wealdstone, Bedford, Kings Lynn and Cambridge City. He finally ended his association with the game when he resigned as coach of Wingate. But at the age of 40, he made his rugby debut on Hackney Marshes in 1975 on the wing for Saracens' eighth team against Old Griffins. 'I liked the actual game but I only got about fives passes in the whole match,' he said at the time. 'If things don't improve I'll have a go at fly-half.'

That was typical of Cliff Jones. He played in the era of the short back and sides, Elvis Presley and soccer supporters with rattles, when football jargon was wing-halves, inside-forwards and big bustling centre-forwards. He played the game for the love of it, an attitude that has become slightly obscured by the massive financial rewards at stake.

CLIFF JONES' PLAYING CAREER

	LEAGUE		F.A. CUP		F.L. CUP		EUROPE		TOTAL	
	App	Gls	App	Gls	App	Gls	App	Gls	App	Gls
1957-58	10	1							10	1
1958-59	22	5	4	2					26	7
1959-60	38	20	4	5					42	25
1960-61	29	15	6	4					35	19
1961-62	38	16	7	4			8	4	53	24
1962-63	37	20	1				6	2	44	22
1963-64	39	14	2				2		43	14
1964-65	39	13	4						43	13
1965-66	9	8	2						11	8
1966-67	20	6	5						25	6
1967-68	30	12	4	1			3	1	37	14
1968-69	7	5			2	1			9	6
	318	135	39	16	2	1	19	7	378	159

WALES: 1958 v Northern Ireland, Hungary, Mexico, Sweden, Hungary, Brazil; 1959 v Northern Ireland, England, Scotland; 1960 v Northern Ireland, Republic of Ireland, Scotland, England; 1961 v Northern Ireland, Spain, Hungary, England, Scotland; 1962 v Northern Ireland, Brazil, Brazil, Mexico, Scotland; 1963 v Hungary, Northern Ireland, England, Scotland; 1964 v Northern Ireland, Scotland, Denmark, England, Greece; 1965 v Greece, Northern Ireland, Italy, USSR; 1966 v Scotland, England; 1967 v England, Scotland; 1968 v West Germany (41 caps).

CHAPTER 6

Alan Gilzean

TOTTENHAM TEAMS DOWN THE DECADES HAVE glittered with exceptional attacking talent. Goalscorers of remarkable international calibre. Quality and quantity in the shape of stars like Jimmy Greaves, Bobby Smith, Martin Chivers, Steve Archibald, and Clive Allen, who scored 49 goals in one season for the club. In the present team there is Gary Lineker, who was crowned the World Cup's top marksman in Mexico in 1986, and who collected four more World Cup Final goals in Italy as he closes in on Greaves' total of 44 England goals.

Lineker, of course, has a world-class pedigree, and had he been a Spurs player for the past 10 years he would probably warrant a place in the all-time greats. I've no doubt that one day he will merit inclusion.

Gilzean may not be in the same league as Lineker in terms of sheer quantity of goals, but his goals were of a rare quality. Once again I am biased toward a player who has provided me with so much personal pleasure through the years at White Hart Lane. As I'm talking as a fan who admired Gilzean from the terraces and the stands, I'm confident in saying my views are shared by thousands of other contemporary Spurs supporters.

Gilzean had the gift to score goals of sheer majesty. His flicks with foot and head were sometimes beyond belief. His goals were made in heaven. He had magic in his boots, and was an artist in the air with that bald head rising to knock the ball in from every conceivable angle.

Wedding day for Alan Gilzean and his bride Irene Todd back in March 1965.

One of the most potent attacking ploys ever seen at White Hart Lane was the long throw of Martin Chivers, headed on by either Alan Gilzean or Mike England. With two such experts in the air, defences found it almost impossible to cope with this strategy.

During my spell as the 'local' Tottenham reporter on the *North London Weekly Herald*, the newspaper ran a highly successful competition to win a number of autographed footballs to be presented on the famous White Hart Lane pitch prior to Gilly's testimonial match against Red Star Belgrade, and such stars as keeper Ojnan Petrovic, striker Vladimar Petrovic and 70-cap Dragan Drajic, a team that knocked Liverpool out of the European Cup the previous season.

One self-conscious, very nervous individual, myself, walked onto the pitch in front of thousands of Gilly's admirers in the stadium with a bag full of balls. Gilzean, the old grey fox of Spurs now with tufts of grey hair above both ears, stood in

The famous 'G' force in action. The 'G-men' were Spurs strikers Jimmy Greaves and Alan Gilzean.

the centre circle handing out the prizes as the proud youngsters' names were announced over the 'tannoy' system.

I didn't know it at the time, as I was totally wrapped up in the presentation, but one fan rushed onto the pitch dodging the stewards and police to fall before Gilly . . . and kiss his boots.

That was a story I missed that was right under my nose! But I feel I had a genuine excuse as I was preoccupied in handing out the *Weekly Herald* prizes. I was standing just a yard from the incident, but I didn't know anything about it until the next day when I saw the picture in the London *Evening News*. I was looking the other way when the fan paid his special homage to Alan Gilzean.

The story is not intended to illustrate my journalistic incompetence, but to demonstrate the sheer affection with which Spurs fans held Alan Gilzean.

Even Bill Nicholson turned out to honour Gilly. It was Nicholson's first match back at White Hart Lane ten weeks after quitting as team boss. It was an emotionally charged night with 22,239 playing £11,000 to say thanks, and to show his appreciation, Gilly gave them a goal in a 2-0 win for Spurs — his 134th and final goal for the club.

One of soccer's outstanding scribes Peter Batt wrote: 'Of all the British footballers I have seen over the past 10 years, Gilzean gave the most highly-personalised entertainment value that could only be matched by the likes of Greaves, Law, and Best . . . We may never see the likes of him again. And, if that isn't worth a tear or two we should all put the shutters up.'

Gilzean also went hand in glove with Greaves. The 'G' men. They were made for each other, Gilzean a sublime provider for Greaves as well as a competent finisher himself.

As partnerships go, Greaves and Bobby Smith or Greaves and Gilzean were perhaps the best of all time at Spurs. Some might go for Smith and Greaves, and they are probably right in terms of the number of goals the pair would have got had they played together longer and both of them at their peak. But for sheer entertainment, my personal choice would be the 'G' men.

It has subsequently transpired that both Gilzean and Greaves shared another passionate interest besides scoring goals for Spurs . . . drinking. Greaves' affliction with alcoholism is well documented and it was also common knowledge that Gilly enjoyed his bacardi and coke.

Terry Venables, as usual, speaks as a fan as well as an expert. He says: 'Alan Gilzean is an artist type. Very slight, deft touches. His heading ability was superb, he had this ability to flick on the ball with amazing skill.

'He was a real craftsman, the type that youngsters would see and say that one day they would like to be like him.'

Sometimes transfers go through smoothly, sometimes they don't. Bill Nicholson endured protracted negotiations before signing Alan Gilzean from Dundee for £72,000, a fee that might have seemed a lot at the time, but today looks like a giveaway for such a talented forward.

'Gilly' takes a smack in the mouth during a match with Ipswich. He may have had a delicate touch but he was also tough.

Gilzean arrived at Spurs at a transitional stage. Dave Mackay had broken his leg for the first time, and Bobby Smith departed to Third Division Brighton for £5,000. Nicholson watched numerous strikers leading up to Christmas 1964 in search of a replacement for Smith before deciding on Gilzean, who had scored some important goals for Dundee in their European Cup run in 1962-3 when they reached the semi-final.

Nicholson recalls: 'From the moment I first asked Bob Shankly, the Dundee manager, for a price, the talks dragged on for three weeks and three times I had to raise my offer. We were in competition with Sunderland, who had offered Gilly more money, and the Italian club Torino, although Gilly told me afterwards he was not interested in going to Italy. Denis Law and Jimmy Greaves had been playing for Italian clubs and Law warned him off.'

Once Nicholson had finally agreed the deal with Dundee, the Spurs boss met the player at an agreed spot on the bank of the River Tay.

'When I met Gilly in his car beside the Tay, he told me he was keen to come to White Hart Lane but Sunderland had offered him £20 for a win and £10 for a draw. "They can't do that," I said. "It's illegal. In the regulations it says a club can only pay £4 for a win and £2 for a draw."

'I must have convinced him I was telling the truth because he rejected Sunderland's offer and accepted my lower one. A few weeks later I met the late Alan Hardaker, Secretary of the Football League, and asked him what clubs were allowed to offer players after the maximum wage restriction was lifted.

'Can they offer money for points?' I asked.

'Yes, they can, providing it's written in the contract,' he replied.

'I was staggered. "But what about the regulations about £4 for a win and £2 for a draw?" I said. "What's the point of having regulations if you don't stick to them?"

'"It's a play on words," answered Hardaker. "Under the new system, you can pay them what you like."

'I told him it might be a good idea if the Football League passed that information on to the clubs.

'I saw Gilly about it a few days later. "I'm afraid I misled you," I said. "I've seen Alan Hardaker and he tells me Sunderland were within their rights to offer you £20 a win."

'I knew I was right,' answered Gilly. Typically of him, he didn't submit a wage claim, but I made sure his contract was improved. The following season we introduced bonuses for points on a sliding scale. The more matches won in succession, the higher the rewards.

'I liked Gilly. He was easy to talk to, never moaned and got on with the job in an uncomplicated way. He was an unorthodox player, different in many ways from Bobby Smith. He was more of a footballing centre forward and started his career as an inside left. He didn't head the ball full on like Smith. He preferred to glance it as he turned his head. It was not a style you could coach in anyone because the margin of error was so small. But it suited him and I never tried to change him.

'Sometimes I would chide him: "Where did you learn your football? What were you trying to do?" He would hit a ball into space up the wing and expect someone to be there to meet it. "If the man is not running, play to feet," I would tell him. "You're not in Scotland now." He would take it in good spirit. I could be open and frank with him and he wouldn't get angry or sulk. He was very trustworthy and likeable. Away from football, he was something of a loner, a quiet, unaggressive man. It was a tribute to his fitness that he was still playing for us at the age of 36. He retired in 1974.

'I never had any problems with Gilly and unlike some of today's footballers, he wasn't greedy when it came to money.

'Before every match he used to soak his boots in hot water to soften them up. I think this was a legacy from the old days when the toe-capped leather boots would be so stiff that they were painful to the feet unless softened up in some way. Some players still did it out of habit.'

Gilzean was sent off against West Ham in September 1966 for arguing with a linesman. The ball appeared to be handled by Bobby Moore and Gilly protested. He had been sent off three times earlier in his career, but there had been no problems by the time he had come to Spurs, and he didn't argue with officials as a rule. After the game Bill Nicholson went to the referee's room and asked Harry New, the Portsmouth referee, why Gilzean had been sent off. The referee reported Nicholson to the FA, but the Spurs manager, who was never in any dispute with soccer's authority, heard no more about it.

Gilzean graduated from a full-time bank clerk and part-time footballer in the tiny Scottish village of Coupar Angus to be hero-worshipped at one of England's most famous clubs.

At the age of 36 he considered himself too old for the demands of League football, but he had a brief flirtation with soccer in South Africa; however, he rejected a two-year contract offered after his first six months at Highland Park, Johannesburg. 'I liked the country, but missed England. It would have been a terrible upheaval to have upped home and moved out there.'

Alan Gilzean does a victory roll, saluted by Martin Peters after a Steve Perryman goal beats Sheffield Wednesday keeper Peter Springett.

He then tried his hand as manager of Southern League club Stevenage. At the time he was working as an executive in a haulage firm. But despite his enormous success as a player, Gilly wasn't really cut out for the demands of football management. After one season the club were bottom of the table and suffering financial nightmares. He said at the time: 'I didn't think there could be so many headaches. The problems of management have been a bit of an eye-opener.' He quit Stevenage over doubts about the club's future.

But Gilly is back at White Hart Lane! His son is a regular in the reserves and has already been called up once by Terry Venables for a taste of the first team when he was called into the squad. Gilly junior is a striker just like his dad.

ALAN GILZEAN'S PLAYING CAREER

	LEAGUE		F.A. CUP		F.L. CUP		EUROPE		TOTAL	
	App	Gls	App	Gls	App	Gls	App	Gls	App	Gls
1964-65	20	11	4	5					24	16
1965-66	40	12	3	3					43	15
1966-67	40	17	8	4					49	21
1967-68	34	8	5				4	2	43	10
1968-69	37	7	4		6				47	7
1969-70	36	10	4						40	10
1970-71	38	9	3	4	7	4			48	17
1971-72	38	11	5	4	4		11	6	58	21
1972-73	35	5	3	1	9	2	9	3	56	11
1973-74	25	3	1		1		4	2	31	5
	343	93	40	21	28	6	28	13	439	133

SCOTLAND: 1965 v Spain, Northern Ireland, Poland, Italy, Wales; 1967 v Wales; 1968 v Austria, Cyprus; 1969 v West Germany, Wales, England, Cyprus, West Germany, Austria; 1970 v Northern Ireland, England; 1971 v Portugal (17 caps).

CHAPTER 7

Bobby Smith

SPURS SUPPORTERS HAVE BEEN SPOILT BY THE quantity of outstanding international strikers.

It is a measure of Bobby Smith's enormous talents that he edges ahead of Martin Chivers, in particular.

With a club like Spurs, with so many notable candidates throughout the ages, a personal selection is bound to arouse debate and disagreement.

For example, Terry Venables' choice would be Chivers rather than Smith. In eight seasons Chivers scored 118 goals in 268 games, but enjoyed two truly remarkable seasons when his power coupled to his finesse made him one of the best forwards in Europe. Regrettably, Chivers did not always fulfil his enormous capabilities, no doubt hampered by serious injury at one stage. He also took the rap, somewhat unfairly, for England's failure against Poland at Wembley which ultimately caused the country's World Cup exit.

Venables prefers to remember Chivers at his very best: when he was in the mood and able to combine his formidable strength with his technical awareness and skills he was almost unstoppable. Venables says: 'He had two purple years. Injury slowed him down to some extent but for two years he was absolutely magnificent, he couldn't stop scoring goals.

'He was world class for two years.'

Absolutely correct, Terry, however, I have got to disagree with his choice, as overall I would go for Smith. My main reason is that Smith played an enormous part in Spurs' Double winning side, and his partnership with Jimmy Greaves was so

Bobby Smith . . . the centre-forward who filled goalkeepers with dread.

productive and effective. In fact for a spell the combination worked just as perfectly for England and the pair scored many goals together for their country.

Venables doesn't underrate Smith's contribution. Venables pays his tribute to Smith: 'He can rightly be labelled as one of the greats. He did it at Spurs for a long time, he was so consistent. He was such a wholehearted player and far more skilful than he was given credit for.'

Once again page the oracle . . . Bill Nicholson delivers his

Bobby Smith and Jimmy Greaves strike partnership was utilised by England. Here Smith is stretchered off at Wembley with words of comfort from Greaves.

expert verdict on battering ram Smith. 'A centre forward always takes punishment but some will take and others will retaliate. Smith would give it back and defenders and goalkeepers were always wary of him. Foreign goalkeepers used to be frightened of him. I do not think it is unfair that a centre forward should adopt this course, providing he is not deliberately fouling. I would remind Smith: 'There will come a time when the bloke who has been giving you stick will be in possession and you can give it him back.' He needed no invitation!

Bobby Smith shows the power of his shooting in 1956.

'Smith was a tough performer. Often he was injured in matches but would insist on playing on. He didn't miss many games. Sometimes his ankles would be so swollen that he could hardly put his boots on but he would still go out. He was crafty about training, sometimes using a bad back as an excuse to avoid it, but by the end of the week he would pronounce himself fit.

'Smith was the best physical-type centre forward of my time. I think it is important to have a player of this style, but it is not a necessity. In the English game the ball tends to be in the air more than it is on the ground and it makes sense to have a big centre forward in the opposing penalty area.'

Bill Nicholson even gave Bobby Smith the edge over the centre forward in his own playing days, Len Duquemin.

Nicholson signed Smith for a mere £15,000 after a five-year spell with Chelsea where Smith rattled in 23 League goals in 74 games.

Smith scored 176 goals in 271 League matches for Spurs, including the opening Cup Final goal in the 67th minute against

Bobby Smith is unmoved by a last desperate tackle as he scores one of the goals that took Spurs to the Double in 1961.

Leicester City at Wembley in 1961 that was to complete the Spurs' glorious Double success, the first Championship and F.A. Cup double this century.

He was Tottenham's Dark Destroyer, the blunt instrument of the mayhem wreaked by the pace of Cliff Jones, the brain of Danny Blanchflower, and the inspirational drive of Dave Mackay.

The son of a north-east miner, Smith played an essential part in a side that most post-war judges still rate above the best of Manchester United, Liverpool and Arsenal.

In 15 England games he scored 13 times, including eight in his first five games.

While Smith was a consistent and efficient goalscorer, Nicholson felt, for the most part, frustrated that Chivers, for many years, failed to live up to all his potential. Nicholson

Two goals down from the first leg, Bobby Smith scored twice in Spurs 8-1 victory over Gornik in the European Cup in September 1961. Trailing 4-2 from the match in Poland, Smith was brought down for Danny Blanchflower to open the scoring from the penalty spot after only eight minutes. After the 10-5 aggregate triumph Smith is mobbed by jubilant Spurs fans.

says: 'In the early '70s Martin Chivers was the best centre forward in England and fully justified his selection for the national side. But there were many occasions when he failed to play up to his reputation. At these times the other players knew he was not producing everything he was capable of and this annoyed them as much as it did me.'

Despite his enormous talent and his huge successes, Smith hit hard times in latter life, indicative of the players of only 20 years ago who failed to gain the sort of financial rewards available to the modern-day stars.

He failed to handle the transition from a £20-a-week maximum wage superstar of his generation to being an unskilled man in the street who turned to painting and decorating to earn a living and then hit rock bottom after a fall down a manhole that left him with an almost crippled left foot.

A great deal was self-imposed poverty after too many visits to the dog tracks and racecourses.

He says: 'I could never tell myself that I was finished. The years just went on and I spent most of them ducking, diving and gambling. I made a bit here and a bit there. Never had a steady job, but I made out as best I could.

'Looking back I never planned ahead. When the day arrived when I was finished as a player, I wasn't ready for it. That's why I cannot blame any lad these days grabbing what he can and setting himself up for life.'

The lifting of the maximum wage came just a little too late for Smith. 'I'd played my part in winning the championship and scored in two winning F.A. Cup Finals in a row, but my wage was still only £30 with £2 for a draw and £4 for a win. When I asked for a rise, they didn't think I deserved one.

'Sure I was bitter. I left Spurs a very unhappy man.'

But again Smith openly admits that he didn't help himself, particularly with his gambling addiction, which even intruded on his playing days.

He admits: 'I had a local bookie hammering at my door once for £500 and Billy Nicholson got to hear of it. That was a lot of money in those days. They were phoned bets and most of it was down to a couple of my team-mates. The bookie came after me because I was the name who played for England. The publicity got a bit nasty but my mates finally settled.

'I used to bet a week's wages on a horse. It doesn't sound a lot now, twenty quid, does it? And, after I had quit playing, I was at the dogs every night and the race tracks too. I was up and down, never losing a fortune and never making one. It became a way of life. I made a few bob here and there. I drove a mini-cab for five years to keep myself going.

'But money came and went. I was a single bloke after getting divorced towards the end of my playing days and all I wanted was a bit of pleasure and to get by. I owned a few dogs and picked up a bit on them round the tracks.'

Smith counted pop star Rod Stewart and Soho strip club

Bobby Smith tests his injured leg before the England team is selected to play the Rest of the World at Wembley in 1963.

owner Paul Raymond among his friends during the height of his fame. 'I played for Rod's charity football team and he once wrote to Spurs asking if he could have the ground for a pop concert and testimonial match for me.

'The Spurs board were a load of old fogies at the time and turned him down. Funny, if the present chairman Irving Scholar had been around, I think he'd have gone for it.

'As it was, I came out of football with £6,000 in the bank. I never blew that gambling, but it's all gone now.'

Smith chuckles at the centre forwards now regarded as the hard men of the front-line attacks, such as John Fashanu and Mick Harford. He says: 'No disrespect to either — they do a good job in a faster game than I knew — but, for toughness, they're not in my league.

'If they are looked on as tough, I can only think I'd have been sent off every week if I played today. Locked up, even.

'My job was to torment people so the others could pick up the pieces. I never retaliated when anyone kicked me. I just bided my time to give them an elbow. Most people I ever played against accepted that if they kicked me, I would kick them back and we got on very well that way.'

It's so sad that Smith ended up disillusioned and hard up. I for one will always remember him for the good times, the exceptional goals and the glory he brought to Spurs. Regrettably an embittered Smith will argue that memories don't pay the bills.

BOBBY SMITH'S PLAYING CAREER

	LEAGUE		F.A. CUP		F.L. CUP		EUROPE		TOTAL	
	App	Gls	App	Gls	App	Gls	App	Gls	App	Gls
1955-56	21	10	6	3					27	13
1956-57	33	18	3	1					36	19
1957-58	38	36	2	2					40	38
1958-59	36	32	4	3					40	35
1959-60	40	25	4	5					44	30
1960-61	36	28	7	5					43	33
1961-62	26	6	4	3			6	6	36	15
1962-63	15	8	1				6	4	22	12
1963-64	26	13	1				2		29	13
	271	176	32	22			14	10	317	208

ENGLAND: 1960 v Northern Ireland, Luxembourg, Spain, Wales; 1961 v Scotland, Portugal; 1962 v Scotland; 1963 v France, Scotland, Brazil, Czechoslovakia, East Germany, Wales, Rest of the World, Northern Ireland (15 caps).

CHAPTER 8

Jimmy Greaves

JIMMY GREAVES . . . SOMEHOW THERE DOESN'T seem anything more to say. Just the name of Greaves conveys enough to Spurs fans, particularly those privileged, like I was, to watch him score goals with such ease and perfection that you are hard pressed to name his goalscoring peer.

Off the field he is just as much an extrovert as he was on it. Yet, whenever Greaves scored he seemed to express himself with remarkable restraint, an almost calm acceptance that he was put on this earth to score goals.

Then, the truth emerged that he was good at other things . . . drinking, for one. Now, he has discovered a new career in television and as an author and newspaper columnist, helped enormously by his 'ghost' writer Norman Giller, ex-*Daily Express* sports reporter.

On the 'Saint and Greavesie' show he is as much loved now by millions as he was admired by thousands of Spurs supporters from the moment he joined the club from AC Milan for a record £99,999 . . . Bill Nicholson refused to make him the first six-figure signing in British football. He needn't have worried about putting too much pressure on Greavesie.

Greaves' biggest disappointment in an illustrious career was to be dropped by former Spurs full-back and England manager in 1966 Alf Ramsey and miss the World Cup Final, his place taken by Liverpool's Roger Hunt. The consolation is that Greaves remains the second-highest England goalscorer of all time with 44, behind Bobby Charlton with 49, and only Gary Lineker likely to challenge either man's record.

Jimmy Greaves finds the net even in a practice match at Roehampton as the England team train for their match against Scotland in 1967.

I know Bill Nicholson would pencil in the name of Ronnie Burgess before any others for his Greatest Ever team . . . for me, it would be the name of Jimmy Greaves.

He scored 220 League goals in 321 appearances. As a fan I would go to White Hart Lane, not hoping for a Jimmy Greaves goal, but expecting one.

Terry Venables relates a classic tale about Greaves. 'I had the privilege of actually playing at two clubs with Jim.

Jimmy Greaves relaxes before another England match, against Spain at Wembley in 1968.

'I had only just got into the Chelsea team, and Greaves was two or three years older but already he was treated like a God. I had played two games, I was 17 years old and Greaves was virtually in a different league . . . he had a pale blue Ford Popular car. He came up to me one day and said, 'I come from Hornchurch, while you come from down the road at Dagenham, would you like a lift, son, to the game? I'll meet you at the end of my road'.

'He was as good as his word and picked me up to take me to the match, but he insisted that we stopped off at Gants Hill for lunch, the same place he always went to.

'I was a bit sheepish and nervous in the company of the great Greaves and when he asked me what I wanted I thought I had better make an impression and order something I felt would be the right sort of pre-match meal. I felt a light bite of boiled chicken would be appropriate before a match.

WILLIAM SHAKESPEARE,
BORN A.D. MDLXIV, DIED MDCXVI.

He glanced from heaven to earth from earth to heaven,
And his imagination bodied forth
The forms of things unknown, and his pencil
Turned them to shape and gave to airy nothing
A local habitation and a name.

He was not of an age, but for all time.
                                    The elements,
So mix'd in him that Nature might stand up,
And say to all the world, this was a man.

Dear son of Memory, great heir of Fame,
A self-raised monument transmits thy name.
Tis not that ought of thee will ever be hid,
. . . .nds a starry-pointing pyramid.

Jimmy Greaves has been recalled to the England team to face Scotland at
Wembley in 1967, and here he poses with a pipe outside the England team
hotel, consulting the 'bard'.

'Greaves ordered roast beef, Yorkshire pudding, roast
potatoes, boiled potatoes, and all the vegetables! He cleared his
plate, and still scored four goals that day against West Brom as
we won by five!'

Venables added: 'After trying to do everything right, I
took another look at my match preparation! Greavsie had just
proved you can be so wrong, yet so right.'

Chris Waddle was sold to Marseille for £4.25 million.
Tony Cottee was bought by Everton for £2,050,000. Gary
Lineker was valued at £2.8 million going from Everton to

Jimmy Greaves meets up with a few old mates in 1986, Bobby Charlton, Denis Law, Gordon Banks, Malcolm Allison and Tony Book.

Barcelona. Ian Rush cost £3 million when sold by Liverpool to Juventus. Paul Gascoigne is valued at £10 million plus. What price Greaves in today's market?

Greaves could have joined Tottenham from school, but chose Chelsea instead. Arthur Rowe was manager at the time. When Nicholson took over he wanted Greaves. He recalls: 'I wanted him from the moment I saw him score his first goal in League football on his Chelsea debut at White Hart Lane. I will never forget it. What a tremendous goal it was! He beat three defenders before stroking the ball into the net. It had the hallmarks of his game, improvisation and genius.'

When Greaves become disillusioned with life in Milan, Nicholson knew he had a good chance of signing him. Some months before Nicholson and Greaves bumped into each other in the most unlikely setting . . . in the men's toilets at the Cafe Royal in Piccadilly when they were both attending a footballing dinner.

'Why didn't you join a better club than Milan?' Nicholson inquired. 'You should have come to Tottenham.' It was meant as light-hearted banter, something to say in the men's toilets. Greaves, always quick with a retort, said: 'I think I will the next time.'

A few weeks later Nicholson took Greaves at his word, certain there were some serious undertones to his chance remark and timing his move well, knowing Greaves was unsettled and ready to return home. A fee of £99,999 was agreed after a considerable amount of haggling and a starting offer of £92,500. Chelsea emerged on the scene determined to re-sign Greaves, but with a ceiling offer of £96,000. Nicholson says: 'It was the most difficult transfer of my career.'

But Nicholson was adamant that he would not pay a six-figure fee, although it was assumed at the time that the fee had been £100,000. He says: 'I refused to make him the first £100,000 footballer, preferring to knock off £1 so that he would not have to carry that label.' Nicholson was very concerned about escalating transfer fees — and he's been proved right.

No-one knows the goalscoring qualities of Jimmy Greaves better than Bill Nicholson . . .

'Greaves had the natural gift of timing. When confronted by the goalkeeper he seemed to be able to whip the ball into the net almost every time, while other forwards in a similar position would often find the keeper making a fine save. Greaves gave the keeper no chance. He rarely blasted the ball, though I did see him score a 20-yarder against Burnley which hit the back of the net at a very high speed.

'The accuracy of his shooting was uncanny. He would appear to pass the ball to the stanchion. His anticipation was first-class. It was as though he was willing the ball to come to him. He had fantastically quick reactions.

'Sometimes the ball would come towards him and you thought the defender who was marking him would get it before he did, but he would stick out a foot and knock it away. Even when he was late, he seemed capable of winning a rebound off his shins and the ball would fall conveniently for him to score. His ratio of success was unmatched.

'There were areas of Greaves' game where he had deficiencies. He wasn't a tackler and didn't much like having to

Former Spurs scoring star Jimmy Greaves discussing tactics during Bill Nicholson's testimonial match at White Hart Lane in 1983.

chase and harass defenders. Nor was he good in the air. He didn't like training but, like so many geniuses, he realised that his gift had to be worked at and he would practise scoring like a golfer practises his swing. Sometimes the other players would complain that he hadn't worked hard enough in a game. 'But he's in the team for his goals,' I would reply. 'Who scored the goal last week? Goalscoring is something you can't all do, but he can do it better than anyone.' Often Alan Gilzean would say at half-time: 'We're going to get nothing out of this game.' And in the 89th minute Jimmy Greaves would pop up and score the winner.

'In his Tottenham career he scored countless memorable goals. One against Leicester when he beat several players before slipping the ball past Peter Shilton remains in the memory, along with a classic against Manchester United. But there were so many.'

Venables also remembers vividly the breathtaking goal against Manchester United at White Hart Lane. He says: 'That is typical of Greaves, the type of goals he scored. They were magnificent. He would weave his way through, and that goal against Manchester United is a particularly good example. He beat three or four defenders and casually passed the ball into the net.

'There isn't much more you can say about Jim. He's a tremendous finisher. A legend here at Tottenham, and quite rightly so.'

The ultimate assessment, inevitably, belongs to Bill Nicholson. 'What I liked about him was his attitude. He was friendly and interested. When I pinned the travel details of a trip on the notice board he would read it thoroughly. He was never late. Most of the other players would scan the bulletin and would be forever inquiring about times.

'Nor did he bear any malice. I had several rows with him over minor matters and there was one occasion when I criticised him for something he had failed to do in the ball court, our indoor training area at the club. He responded angrily and there was silence as the other players stopped to listen. It was one of the most explosive moments of my career. Yet next morning when he came in he was as cheerful as ever.

'I was amazed some years later to hear of his revelations about drink and how he became an alcoholic. I must say he never gave me any reason to suspect that he had a problem. It certainly never interfered with his football, or lessened his professionalism.'

Greaves quit the game far too early, at the age of 31. The 1966 World Cup was described by Nicholson as a 'watershed' for Greaves. Injured early on in the tournament, by the time he got fit Roger Hunt was established as Geoff Hurst's partner in attack. He also contracted hepatitis, a very debilitating illness for an athlete.

Suspecting that his reactions had slowed because of the illness and with Greaves concentrating more on his outside business interest, Nicholson took the opportunity to swap him for Martin Peters. Nicholson agreed a £200,000 transfer for

Now a TV star with his own programme 'Saint and Greavesie'.

Peters with West Ham manager Ron Greenwood with Greaves accounting for £54,000. Greaves stayed less than two seasons with West Ham United before announcing his retirement. Nicholson says: 'He was a proud man and when he realised that his gift of being able to score remarkable goals was forsaking him he quit.'

He came out of retirement a few years later to play non-league football for Barnet because he was still in love with the game and probably came to realise that he had left the game prematurely.

Nicholson says: 'If anyone was unique in the world of football it was him . . . he was one of the best goalscorers of all time.'

It was such a shock to the system to discover that such a wonderful talent was later tarnished. For some reason you expect your heroes to be perfect. And, of course they are not. Still, it comes as quite a surprise when the truth finally emerges.

In his latest book, *It's A Funny Old Life,* the 50-year-old

TV star reveals his fight against alcoholism, the devastating effect on his family, on his marriage. But he reveals that Irene's decision in divorcing him saved his life by finally bringing him to his senses, and they are back together again, living with each other, and touchingly his new autobiography is dedicated to his 49-year-old partner.

JIMMY GREAVES' PLAYING CAREER

	LEAGUE		F.A. CUP		F.L. CUP		EUROPE		TOTAL	
	App	Gls	App	Gls	App	Gls	App	Gls	App	Gls
1961-62	22	21	7	9			2		31	30
1962-63	41	37	1				6	5	48	42
1963-64	41	35	2				2	1	45	36
1964-65	41	29	4	6					45	35
1965-66	29	15	2	1					31	16
1966-67	38	25	8	6	1				47	31
1967-68	39	23	4	3			4	3	47	29
1968-69	42	27	4	4	6	5			52	36
1969-70	29	8	4	3	1				34	11
	322	220	36	32	8	5	14	9	380	266

ENGLAND: 1962 v Scotland, Switzerland, Peru, Hungary, Argentina, Bulgaria, Brazil, France, Northern Ireland, Wales; 1963 v France, Scotland, Brazil, Czechoslovakia, Switzerland, Wales, Rest of the World, Northern Ireland; 1964 v Uruguay, Portugal, Republic of Ireland, Brazil, Portugal, Argentina, Northern Ireland, Belgium, Holland; 1965 v Scotland, Hungary, Yugoslavia, Wales, Austria; 1966 v Yugoslavia, Norway, Denmark, Poland, Uruguay, Mexico, France; 1967 v Scotland, Spain, Austria (42 caps).

CHAPTER 9

Pat Jennings

PAT JENNINGS WAS AWARDED THE OBE FOR HIS services to football after retiring at the end of the 1986 World Cup Finals in Mexico where he made the last of his record-breaking 119 appearances for Northern Ireland against Brazil on June 12 — his 41st birthday.

During his astonishing, illustrious 23-year career, Jennings made 757 League appearances for Watford, Spurs and Arsenal, appearing in more than 1,000 first-class games.

Terry Venables has pleaded for forgiveness in leaving the ever-so-popular Pat Jennings out of his personal choice for an all-time great Spurs team. Instead, he surprisingly opted for his boyhood idol Ted Ditchburn. The Spurs manager launched the video of his Great Team selection in a West London hotel at a press conference hosted by the highly professional, knowledgeable, and likeable TV commentator Brian Moore who said: 'It has been a very difficult task for the Spurs manager . . . but it is disgraceful that he has left out Pat Jennings!'

Venables explains: 'I know I will be very unpopular going for Ted Ditchburn. Pat is a great bloke and a fantastic goalkeeper.

'Pat, please forgive me!'

I'm sorry, Tel, Pat may have a forgiving nature, but I can't forgive you.

The reason is simple: Pat Jennings will forever remain one of my all-time idols, a great player and a gentleman.

His extraordinary one-handed saves as he plucked the ball

out of the air were breathtaking, a legacy of his days in Gaelic football.

Venables recognised his rare talent when he says: 'Those big hands were able to cope well, but those saves are not in the footballing manual, you couldn't and shouldn't teach such methods as they are basically unsafe.

'But Pat had a slightly longer reach that enabled him to make those one-handed saves with a huge degree of safety.

'Knowing Pat, they were not a sign of any flashness, but something only he was able to do. It is a gift that only one of the true greats would have.'

Yet, Terry chose Ted Ditchburn instead. Why? 'Well, he was in goal when I first started watching Tottenham. He was incredible, so good he dominated the whole team. I saw him make three or four saves I just couldn't believe, but I suppose in those days, without TV, you were the star in your street when you actually went to see the match and would come back and relate the wonderful stories of all the action.

'I saw a lot of Bill Brown, and he was a great shot stopper, but Ted Ditchburn was one of my all-time favourite players.'

Even Bill Nicholson has a problem separating the great goalkeeping talents of Jennings and Ditchburn. He argues: 'I find it impossible to choose between the two. It is the same kind of dilemma that confronted Ron Greenwood when he became England manager in 1977: should he choose Peter Shilton or Ray Clemence? I can appreciate the problem. I would take the coward's way out and put the names of both Jennings and Ditchburn on my team sheet and go missing until Saturday afternoon, hoping that one of them forgot to turn up!

'Ted Ditchburn was a colossus. Like Jennings, he was tremendous at coming off his line and was also brave at going down at the feet of forwards. His reflexes were astonishing and though we complained about his kicking, none of us worried too much about it. Jennings had similar qualities to Ditchburn — quick and brave and his reactions were equally good.'

Pat Jennings held the world record number of international appearances until Peter Shilton took over in the 1990 World Cup Finals.

But when it finally came to the crunch Bill Nicholson chose Jennings ahead, albeit fractionally, of Ted Ditchburn.

Jennings was transferred from Newry Town to Watford for a fee of £6,500 on the advice of a former Irish international Billy McClacken, who was 79 years old when he saw Jennings playing for an Irish Youth side at Bromley. After a season and 52 games at Vicarage Road, Jennings joined Tottenham in June 1964 for £27,000 and, three years later, won his first F.A. Cup medal when Spurs defeated Chelsea 2-1 at Wembley. He gained his second when Arsenal achieved a 3-2 win over Manchester United in 1979.

Although Jennings enjoyed a second career with Arsenal, his best years were at Spurs.

Pound for pound Jennings was one of Nicholson's best-ever signings at £27,000 as a replacement for Bill Brown in 1964. He signed for Spurs at the age of 19.

Nicholson recalls: 'The signing of Pat proved to be one of my most successful signings because he was to stay at White Hart Lane for 13 years and reach the very highest class as a goalkeeper.

'I do not claim he was the number one in Britain during his best years with us, but I know there was no one better. At this level, the top class, there is little to choose between players like Shilton, Clemence, and Jennings. What I liked about Pat was his calm, steadying influence. Before a game he would be one of the most keyed-up players in the dressing room, but out on the field he gave the appearance of being the most controlled. I like players to reveal signs of tension before a match. It shows that total attention is being given to the task ahead.'

Oddly enough Pat Jennings made a very shaky start to his Spurs career, and it might have crossed Bill Nicholson's mind to sell him.

He says: 'In his first year with us Pat was too tense, too nervous. He hardly opened his mouth and two seasons went by before he established himself in the side and forced Brown out. After a bad game I left him out, which didn't help his confidence. I had to appeal to the supporters through the local Press to stop pillorying him when he played and give him a chance. He was replacing an idol in Bill Brown and they weren't willing to encourage him. A number of players, including Mullery and Venables, were to find similar problems with our crowd. The people who barracked were probably the same people who complained when Jennings left Tottenham in 1977 to join Arsenal!

'Perhaps I put him in too early. I was wary as a rule about introducing young players too soon. There is a chance they will fall as quickly as they have risen. It is better to give them a cautious start. But in Pat's case, he had already played two games for Northern Ireland and was hardly a beginner.'

Nicholson recalls how he pulled off the transfer for Jennings. 'I had seen him play on a number of occasions and when I rang Bill McGarry, the Watford manager, about him he said: 'If you get him, you'll be on a winner.' Watford were desperately short of money and I knew McGarry would not stand in Pat's way. I had a setback at first when Jennings rejected my offer of £38-a-week. He said he was receiving that

Pat Jennings with his OBE for services to football.

at Vicarage Road. But once McGarry had made it clear that he didn't want him to stay, he accepted a revised offer of £40-a-week plus £5 for each first-team appearance.'

Once Jennings settled in at Spurs, successfully overcoming his early jitters, he became one of the world's top keepers.

Nicholson adds: 'Pat weighed just over 13 stone and was built like Peter Shilton. That's important for a goalkeeper. He needs a bulky physique to enable him to go for high balls in a congested area. Ray Clemence has disproved this theory, but in

Pat Jennings holds some of the top individual awards, including the Player's Player of the Year trophy and the Football Writer's Player of the Year trophy.

general the lighter the build of a goalkeeper, the more likely he is to be bundled off the ball. Pat was a great jumper, which is another vital aspect of the job. Sometimes, however, he would be reluctant to come for crosses. He would stay on his line and expect the centre half to clear the ball. With someone like Mike England in the side this often worked, but there were times it didn't. I arranged a session for the other players to bombard Pat with crosses and by the end of it he had regained his confidence.'

Goalkeepers have been sent off, some have poor disciplinary records, and there is even the case of GBH by West German keeper Harold Schumaker against Frenchman

The family man. At home with wife Eleanor and the children.

Battison in the World Cup Finals. But Jennings was the perfect gentleman on the field, had the ideal temperament, and was never provoked . . . except once.

Nicholson recalls: 'The only time I saw Pat Jennings lose his temper was in a match against Leeds at Elland Road in 1968. It was the first and only time Pat was cautioned in more than 1,000 matches. Five days earlier Tottenham had ended the Leeds unbeaten run of 26 matches at White Hart Lane and Revie's team was intent on revenge. Every time Pat went for the ball, a Leeds player crashed into him. Brought up in the tough world of Gaelic football in Newry, Pat wasn't too bothered at first. But by half-time he had been knocked down

Pat Jennings proved he has a sense of humour — he signed for Arsenal!

half a dozen times without being given much protection by the referee, Peter Baldwin, and was becoming annoyed. In the 63rd minute Mick Jones, the Leeds centre forward, collided with him again and, as they lay on the ground, the two men had their legs entangled. Pat tried to get up but couldn't. Eventually they scrambled clear and stood glaring at each other. Perhaps thinking that Jennings was about to hit him, Jones threw a punch and caught Pat on the chin. As Jones

Total concentration, dedication, and supreme fitness coupled with his exceptional talents kept him going until the age of 41.

turned away, Pat went after him and kicked him in the rear! A linesman spotted it and waved his flag. Acting on the linesman's advice, the referee cautioned Pat and awarded a penalty! Dave Mackay was so annoyed that when Peter Lorimer put the ball on the penalty spot, he kicked it into our net. He was not cautioned as perhaps he would have been today. Lorimer converted the spot-kick and we lost the game.

'Later on, we had Alan Gilzean sent off after a clash with Terry Cooper, the Leeds left back. I was furious. I told Jennings that he was at fault for falling for the bait. Leeds had been trying to goad him into retaliating and he should have known better. But I still felt sorry for him.'

Generally Pat Jennings avoided controversy, he never courted the headlines, in fact he shunned them. But his departure from Spurs was not an amicable one.

After 13 years with Spurs, manager Keith Burkinshaw sold him to Arsenal for £45,000. Pat had played a record number of games, later to be surpassed by Steve Perryman, but the manager felt that Jennings was reaching the end of his career at the age of 32, while his understudy Barry Daines was 26 and was fed up hanging around in the great man's shadow. Jennings was also negotiating a new contract: with one year left he could have walked out of Spurs on a free transfer taking advantage of a League rule; any player with five years' continual service after the age of 33 would be entitled to a free transfer. The manager opted to let Jennings go and keep Daines. Spurs fans were far from happy at Jennings switching to Highbury, particularly as he played on for many years still an outstanding keeper, while at White Hart Lane a succession of keepers came and went but failed to fill his boots, until Keith Burkinshaw paid Liverpool £300,000 for England international Ray Clemence who, ironically, arrived at White Hart Lane at the age of 33, a year older than when Jennings left.

Jennings ended his outstanding career at the highest possible level in the World Cup Finals with Northern Ireland. But he knew he was not cut out for the pressure-cooker atmosphere of coaching and management, so he didn't try. 'Bigger names than mine have been lost to football. I've had a lot of offers since I officially retired. I've been asked to coach in America and Australia and I've had offers to go into management in England. With my name, the pressure would be right on me. I like the idea of coaching, but not all the pressure that goes with it.'

Jennings contents himself with numerous personal appearances and is still a regular visitor to his beloved Tottenham where he spent '13 happy and successful years.'

A 25,000 crowd at Windsor Park, Belfast, paid tribute to Jennings. The Jennings Select XI included George Best, who made his debut with Jennings for Northern Ireland against Wales at Swansea in 1964.

The Times wrote: 'Jennings has bestrode the world stage with a dignity and modesty that placed him on a pedestal few mortals ever achieve. If there is a grain of truth in the hackneyed phrase "a true ambassador for his sport and country", then it applies to Jennings. That doyen of wing halves from another era, Danny Blanchflower, whose simplistic style and elegance made him quite unique as a player, said of Jennings in one of many tributes: "Not only did he survive in the big time, but he mastered it. He became one of the greatest with his cool, smooth, style."

'It is never too difficult in most cases, if one probes beneath the surface, to discover something of an unsavoury nature in many of those who make newspaper headlines. In truth, in many instances there is no need to probe. Not so with Jennings. His conduct on and off the field has been exemplary and the youth of today have in him a perfect example of all that portrays true sportsmanship.'

PAT JENNINGS' PLAYING CAREER

	LEAGUE		F.A. CUP		F.L. CUP		EUROPE		TOTAL	
	App	Gls	App	Gls	App	Gls	App	Gls	App	Gls
1964-65	23								23	
1965-66	22		3						25	
1966-67	41		8		1				50	
1967-68	42		5				4		51	
1968-69	42		4		6				52	
1969-70	42		4		1				47	
1970-71	40		5		6				51	
1971-72	41		5		7		12		65	
1972-73	40		3		10		10		63	
1973-74	36		1				10		47	
1974-75	41		2		1				44	
1975-76	40		2		6				48	
1976-77	23		1		1				25	
	473		43		39		36		591	

NORTHERN IRELAND: 1964 v England, Switzerland, Switzerland, Scotland; 1965 v Holland, Albania, Scotland, England, Albania; 1966 v Wales, West Germany, England, Scotland; 1967 v Scotland, England; 1968 v Wales, Israel, Turkey, Turkey; 1969 v England, Scotland, Wales, USSR, USSR; 1970 v Scotland, England; 1971 v Cyprus, Cyprus, England, Scotland, Wales, USSR; 1972 v Spain, Scotland, England, Wales, Bulgaria; 1973 v Cyprus, Portugal, England, Scotland, Wales, Portugal; 1974 v Scotland, England, Wales, Norway, Sweden; 1975 v Yugoslavia, England, Scotland, Wales, Sweden, Norway, Yugoslavia; 1976 v Israel, Scotland, England, Wales, Holland, Belgium; 1977 v West Germany, England, Scotland, Wales, Iceland; 1985 v Turkey, Rumania, England; 1986 v France, Denmark, Morocco, Algeria, Spain, Brazil (75 caps).

CHAPTER 10

Ossie Ardiles

'**O**SVALDO ARDILES POSSESSES A WORLD CUP winners medal, and F.A. Cup winners medal and was arguably the most stylish player in the First Division during the 1980s'. That is a recent description of the Swindon Town manager, Ossie Ardiles, by the *Daily Telegraph*.

They went on: 'Twenty years ago, "Ossie" meant Peter Osgood, the Chelsea forward who became one of many outstanding club players never to have transferred his skills to the international scene. Now, Ossie means Ardiles.'

Ossie Ardiles and Glenn Hoddle are the only modern-day players to earn selection for the Top Ten Tottenham All-Time Greats. That is a tribute to Spurs' glorious past, rather than any indictment of the current crop of talent.

'Thank you very much' was Ossie's instant reaction when I told him of his selection. 'It is an honour to be in such company with so many great Spurs players.' He has always been extremely polite. He has also been widely acclaimed as the most successful of the hundreds of foreign imports since he opened the floodgates in 1978 along with his compatriot Ricky Villa.

He is surprised that only Glenn Hoddle and himself warrant inclusion in the all-time Spurs Greats, not knowing intimately the wealth of talent in the club's glorious past.

He said: 'Glenn Hoddle was the only player I really knew at Spurs at this level. It was a privilege for me to play alongside him for nine years. He was a wonderfully gifted player for Spurs.'

Ossie Ardiles with wife Sylvia and son Frederico in 1982.

Ardiles sat in his manager's office at Swindon Town reflecting on his Spurs career: 'I was very proud to be part of a great, great footballing team in the early '80s and to have played in the 1981 F.A. Cup Final. We also won the Cup the following season, played Liverpool in the final of the Littlewoods Cup and beat Barcelona in Europe.'

Ossie was so popular that there is a famous line in the Spurs Cup Final song, which made the 'Top Ten', recorded by Chas and Dave . . . 'Ossie's going to Wembley, his knees have gone all trembly.'

Ardiles went on: 'I thoroughly enjoyed my time there, and it was a privilege to watch so many changes take place as the club moved on from being a family club to big business.

'I consider Spurs to be not just one of the best clubs in English football, but one of the best clubs in the world.

'Ossie' knows how to celebrate a goal for his beloved 'Tott-ing-ham'.

Osvaldo Ardiles acknowledges the crowd at the River Plate Stadium before the Argentinian-Soviet Union match in 1982.

'Ever since I arrived at Spurs with my friend Ricky Villa in 1978 the fans took us to their hearts, it's as simple as that. I shall always have a place in my heart for those Spurs supporters.'

Terry Venables has no doubts about his status as a Spurs player. 'Ossie Ardiles will go down as one of the Tottenham greats'.

Ardiles reached the end of his illustrious Spurs career just as Venables took charge after leaving Barcelona. But Venables has studied the qualities of the little Argentinian, who is the proud owner of a World Cup winners' medal in '78. 'Ossie is one of the best close dribblers and controllers of the ball I've seen.

'It was a shame that he couldn't score more goals, but he often set them up for other people.

'He was a strong little fellow. He possessed the technique

Sensation in 1978. Two World Cup winners, Ricky Villa and Osvaldo Ardiles, sign for Spurs. Villa and his pregnant wife, 21-year-old Christina, and Ardiles arrive at Gatwick Airport.

to screen the ball, hold off people with his arms stretched out, a skill developed in a lot of South American countries.

'He was very, very good for Glenn Hoddle. He freed Glenn Hoddle with his passing, eliminating opponents out of the game by supplying Glenn with the ball.

'He was a great player for Tottenham but one thing that helped Ossie settle down was, of course, having his great pal Ricky Villa with him.

'Villa was not that successful early on, while Ossie did better even at the beginning, but he was capable of incredible individualistic things. For a big man, Ricky Villa had fast feet, capable of taking opponents on, and nothing highlighted that more than his great Cup Final goal against Manchester City. That must go down as one of the all-time great goals scored for this club.'

Ardiles suffered the anguish of split loyalties when the Falklands War broke out. His two boys were born in England and considered their Hertfordshire house their natural 'home'. They had even begun to speak with a sharp Cockney accent.

The dynamic midfield duo Ossie Ardiles and Glenn Hoddle on the eve of the 1982 Milk Cup Final with Liverpool.

Throughout his personal ordeal, Ardiles, who had come to this country as a qualified lawyer, conducted himself with dignity, diplomacy, sensitivity, and compassion.

He recalls: 'The War was very tough on me. There was a lot of pressure from everywhere, and sometimes I thought life would be simpler if I just went back to Argentina. People from home considered me a kind of traitor for playing here, for being friendly with English people. But the war was over, so I stayed.'

He was able to return and still be accepted. He has moved into management with Swindon, shunning offers to return to his native Argentina. His long-term ambitions are to return to both Spurs and Argentina as manager.

As a player he placed the emphasis on skill. He always wondered why Glenn Hoddle was not an automatic choice for England and called Diego Maradona his personal friend. In

Ossie Ardiles opened the floodgates for foreign stars in 1978 and he has been the best of all the imports.

fact, Maradona came to London to make a guest appearance in Ossie's testimonial match at White Hart Lane.

South American players have been stereotyped as play-actors, feigners of injury, or hard-men. Ardiles was none of

Ossie Ardiles scores a superb goal against Manchester United at White Hart Lane and striker Chris Jones offers his congratulations.

these. Bill Nicholson considered him one of the game's 'gentlemen' in common with Trevor Brooking. It was Nicholson who first got the call alerting Spurs that the two Argentinians were available.

'On Thursday, 29 June 1978, I received a phone call from an old friend of many years' standing, which was to have a great effect on Tottenham. Harry Haslam was manager of Sheffield United at the time. He said that Oscar Arce, an Argentinian coach on his staff, had alerted him to the fact that two of the Argentine players who had helped their country win the World Cup for the first time four days previously, Osvaldo Ardiles and Ricardo Villa, wanted to come to England to play for a top club.

'Sheffield United were interested, but Harry said: "The deal will cost about £400,000 and we don't have that kind of money. It's got to be a big club like yours, or Arsenal." He felt that Tottenham, having just been re-promoted to the First Division, needed players of this quality to make an impact in

'Ossie's' great dream was to play at Wembley and he fulfilled it, playing in the F.A. Cup Final.

their first season back. I agreed with him. I had seen Ardiles on television and had been impressed by him. He was obviously a player who would improve our side. I hadn't seen so much of Villa. He had come on as substitute in two games, but was not a front-line player.

'Harry assured me that Villa was highly rated in

Argentinian football. Antonio Rattin, captain of the Argentine side that played England at Wembley in 1966, had given him a strong personal recommendation.'

Rattin will always be remembered in this country for his World Cup disgrace at Wembley. He was sent off. The conduct of his team provoked Sir Alf Ramsey into calling the Argentinians 'animals'.

Nicholson went on: 'Rattin was now a businessman in Buenos Aires and was handling the negotiations from that end.

'When my telephone conversations with Harry had finished, I went to see Keith Burkinshaw to tell him the news. Keith was as excited as I had been. A meeting of the directors was going on that day and he went to see chairman Sidney Wale to find out whether the club would be prepared to find the necessary money. Mr Wale said he was willing for talks to start. He recognised the value of having two World Cup players on Tottenham's books.

'Harry told me that he had rung Terry Neill, the Arsenal manager, and that Arsenal were considering making a bid. He also said that Manchester City had made contact but had dropped out; the club didn't have the cash. Keith Burkinshaw decided to fly out to Buenos Aires once he had the backing of the board. I am told that he took only 20 minutes to finalise terms with Ardiles and his talks with Villa took not much longer. Both players were desperately keen to come to London. Ardiles spoke a little English, but was an intelligent man who would have no problems. Villa spoke hardly any.

'There was a worry that it might prove difficult to obtain work permits but that obstacle was soon overcome. The Professional Footballers Association was concerned that the import of foreign players would deny opportunities to their members and mean that money was going out of the country, but I am sure their officials would concede now that Ardiles and Villa contributed enormously to English football both by the way in which they played and the dignified manner in which they conducted themselves. Any aspiring midfield player would have learned a lot from playing with or against Ardiles, or even watching him.

'Though a small man, he was quick and brave and his passing, particularly when under pressure, was an object lesson. His balance was such that he could ride most tackles and still find a way through the tightest of defences. He was an artist and there haven't been too many of those playing in English football in recent years. Sadly, after he returned from his exile with Paris St. Germain, he was seriously injured and his form suffered. He wasn't the same player, but I will never forget what he did when he was at his peak and I am sure that most Tottenham fans share my sense of appreciation.

'Both Ardiles and Villa were wonderful characters, warm and friendly, and it was regrettable that Ossie was booed whenever he played after the Falklands War.'

Anti-British views had wrongly been attributed to him in some Argentinian newspapers and a minority of English fans barracked him as a result. The first F.A. Cup Final in which he took part, against Manchester City in 1981, was televised live in Argentina but by the time Tottenham were back at Wembley to play QPR a year later, Argentina had invaded the Falklands and Ossie was in Buenos Aires training with Cesar Menotti's World Cup squad. 'Ricky Villa had to be left out of the side against QPR and not having two of our best players undoubtedly affected the quality of the match.'

Only the import of the two Dutchmen by Bobby Robson at Ipswich, Frans Thijssen and Arnold Muhren, can compare with the successful Spurs duo, and Ardiles in particular.

Yet, when Ardiles and Villa first arrived in the First Division there were many cynics who felt they wouldn't last until Christmas!

Ardiles says: 'There were definitely many people who didn't think I would stand up to the rigours of English football.'

It is interesting that it should be Spurs who began the import of foreign players in 1978 with Ardiles and Villa, who in

1989 would win their battle to increase the number of players qualified to play from two to three, a new regulation brought in by Spurs chairman Irving Scholar, having been defeated the previous year at the League's AGM.

And, despite his enforced break in French football because of the Falklands, Ardiles was considered to have qualified for five years' unbroken service with Spurs and was no longer labelled a 'foreign' import.

He played out his career with a loan period at Blackburn and a move to QPR before securing the post as manager of Swindon. He wanted to qualify as a full FA coach, but at first the narrow-minded at the FA refused him permission, but after persuasion from the players' union the FA, quite rightly, relented.

Born in Cordoba on August 3, 1952, Ardiles began his football career with Huracan in 1970 and played for them for eight years. He won the fans' affection with his love for Tottenham. As the *Sunday Times* said of him: 'For a decade he has been the Argentinian we have most admired, a man of tiny physique but towering soccer sophistication, bringing calm to England's frenzied League play. While all about him charged in ever-decreasing circles, Ossie would put a foot on the ball, find space, direct a colleague and set Spurs rolling. Never before had a Latin played among us for so long or exuded such joy. The Falklands War notwithstanding, we had the prime of Ardiles after he had risen from playing in the streets of Cordoba to be the hub of the Argentinian team that won the 1978 World Cup. What a tribute it is to our way of life and our football that he seems to make the transition from player to manager in England.'

Ardiles would be a popular choice to eventually succeed Terry Venables. He is a rare commodity: an intellectual in football. 'Few, if any, have entertained us with greater charm throughout their playing careers and remained as true to their principles when managers than Ardiles', wrote *The Times*.

Ardiles lists Aristotle as the historical figure he most

Not even the Falklands War diminished the affection he generates from Spurs supporters and admiration from the whole football-loving country.

identifies with. 'He was a logical man and I admire him.' Mozart, The Beatles and listening to his son Fede play the guitar are his favourite musical recreations, while Graham Greene and Jorge Luis Borges are his favourite writers. When asked, 'Which living person do you most admire?' he answered: 'Mother Teresa, Gorbachev; in football, Gary Mabbutt.' That gives you some idea of the man. His favourite pastime is golf, but his ideal of perfect happiness is 'sitting next to the fire, eating popcorn or pizza, with my wife Sylvia, my two sons Pablo and Federico and my two Yorkshire terriers.' His happiest memory is winning the World Cup, naturally. And his favourite building? Well, it had to be Wembley.

Of course, no-one is perfect, and he does profess to having one bad habit. He smokes between ten to fifteen cigarettes a day, in the manner of his mentor Menotti, but unlike the man who took Argentina to the World Cup triumph, it's never in front of his strictly non-smoking team. 'I don't ever smoke in the dug-out during a match. Sometimes I am tempted but you will never see me doing that because it is a bad example.'

OSSIE ARDILES' PLAYING CAREER

	LEAGUE		F.A. CUP		F.L. CUP		EUROPE		TOTAL	
	App	Gls	App	Gls	App	Gls	App	Gls	App	Gls
1978-79	38	3	5	1	2				45	4
1979-80	40	3	6	2	1				47	5
1980-81	36	5	7	1	6	1			49	7
1981-82	26	2	5		8	1	6	1	45	4
1982-83	2		1		1				4	
1983-84	9		1				3	1	13	1
1984-85	11	2							11	2
1985-86	23	1	2		4				29	1
1986-87	24		4		7				35	
1987-88	28		1		3	1			33	1
	237	16	32	4	32	3	9	2	311	25

ARGENTINA: 1981 v West Germany, Brazil; 1982 v Belgium, Hungary, El Salvador, Italy, Brazil (7 caps).

CHAPTER 11

Glenn Hoddle

I'VE GOT TO OWN UP TO CONSIDERABLE BIAS AS far as Glenn Hoddle is concerned. I've been entranced by his football for a decade. I'm a Glenn Hoddle convert.

No doubt that is grossly unfair on past generations of soccer geniuses to have graced White Hart Lane, but Hoddle is the King, in my book!

While I was reared on the talents of the Double team and marvelled at the skills of the stars of the late '60s, Hoddle was the player I could appreciate most in my formative years.

'Hoddle, Hoddle . . . born is the King of White Hart Lane' sang the Tottenham fans, and I would agree with them. They transferred one of their favourite verses from Alan Gilzean to Hoddle, and few players deserved it more.

Hoddle was a player who divided a nation. Should he play for England or shouldn't he? Was he a luxury or one of the most gifted players of his generation to stand comparison alongside Michel Platini as a world-class performer? As far as I'm concerned there is no debate. Hoddle should have been the cornerstone of the England team so that when it came to World Cups and European Championships he would have been the midfield fulcrum, the undisputed No. 1 playmaker, for the England side. Instead, there was always a suspicion that even Bobby Robson picked him on sufferance, perhaps not at first, when Robson was sure Hoddle deserved a run in the team. It was consistently demanded of Hoddle that he had to conform to a team pattern. Yet, no-one would dare suggest the same of the great Frenchman, Platini.

Glenn Hoddle turned his talents to singing with Chas and Dave. He even tried to dress in similar fashion along with team-mate Ray Clemence.

What a shame Hoddle's exceptional skills were only really appreciated once he left these shores for the millionaire's tax haven of Monte Carlo. I'm afraid no England manager, at least the two who had the chance — Ron Greenwood and Robson — had the courage to gamble with Hoddle as the centrepiece of their team. Once he arrived in Monaco, the coach, Arsene Wenger, handed Hoddle the strings to his entire team. 'Win the ball and give it to Hoddle' was his simple philosophy. It took Monaco to the Championship.

Terry Venables had no hesitation in selecting Hoddle for his Greatest Ever Tottenham Team. His reasons: 'His feet are like hands! He can bring the ball down with his feet as if he was using his hands even when there are three defenders surrounding him, and you would think "that's it, he can't get out of it". Platini was very much like Glenn, he couldn't tackle back but no-one gave him the sort of criticism that Glenn had to suffer.

The 1982 version of Glenn Hoddle and proud to have become an England international.

'Lots of things have been said about Glenn Hoddle; lots of good things, lots of derogatory things, lots of things he couldn't do, and I never understand that. I thought he was possibly as talented a one-touch player, two-touch or 100 touches, as I have ever seen. He was just extremely, extremely talented.

'But there were things they said Glenn couldn't do, and

Glenn became aware of it, perhaps spending too much time worrying about it, always trying to prove people wrong and fighting against it. To get the best out of Glenn, as in most things in life, you have to concentrate on his strengths. You wouldn't get the best out of him while he was heading the ball off his own goal-line! The sad thing is that he didn't deserve some of the criticism he got.'

Hoddle scored some sensational goals, and Venables was delighted that one of his best was reserved for a 'farewell' performance against Oxford at White Hart Lane when he dribbled the ball past the entire defence, starting from inside his own half before sending the keeper the wrong way for a glorious goal.

'It was theatrical,' enthused Venables. 'He ran the length of the field, past one defender, past another, and inevitably putting the ball in the back of the net as if to say "thanks for everything".

'I was so glad that was the way it ended for him at Tottenham. He was one of the legends of the club.'

Personally, I always felt that Hoddle's lack of real pace, rather than his failure to chase back and tackle, held him back from becoming one of the world's truly outstanding players.

Of course his main quality was his exceptional passing ability, and he could play backspin on the ball like a golfer chipping to the green. He passed the ball from every conceivable angle. Bill Nicholson likened him to Johnny Haynes.

Hoddle scored some wonderful goals for Spurs, astonishing goals, wonder-goals. Perhaps among the most memorable was his angled sideways-on volleyed strike against Liverpool, captured by TV and often repeated. His chip over the Watford keeper from an incredible angle as he turned and fell was another goal often repeated on television. He had the skills of a Brazilian or, indeed, a Platini, when it came to free kicks, and scored some excellent goals from this position.

I can remember his very first goal for Spurs on his full

Winning an aerial challenge against Roy Aitken in a Hampden Park clash with Scotland in 1978.

debut at Stoke, beating Peter Shilton with a long-range shot that hardly moved more than a foot off the ground . . . I was there. And, I just knew that was the start of a career worth watching. He scored on his England debut at Wembley with a deliberate sidefoot shot on the edge of the box against Bulgaria — then he was dropped for the next match by Greenwood!

For those who felt he wasn't brave, he carries the scars to this day of some horrific head wounds, one in particular at Wembley when he came back with his head bandaged and his forehead stitched.

Off the field, Hoddle matured into a highly respected individual, one of the true Gentlemen of Soccer, in line with Trevor Brooking and Pat Jennings. I had the privilege to ghost write his autobiography *Born Is The Spur* in which he emerged as a compassionate human being, as well as having the courage to reveal his genuine and complete discovery of his true faith in God.

Hoddle loved his music. He spent hours in Mexico during the 1986 World Cup Finals listening to his 'Walkman' by the pool before and after matches. He even made a hit song with his pal Chris Waddle. Waddle took over Hoddle's mantle in the team and the fans' affections once Hoddle departed for French football.

Waddle enjoyed his best season once freed from Hoddle's shadow and with the responsibility of carrying the team. Waddle joined Hoddle in France, his move to Marseilles coming at a time when Waddle had established himself at White Hart Lane, but the £4.25 million fee was too much for Spurs to turn down, and the £2 million contract too tempting for the player to ignore. Perhaps, had Waddle stayed, he would have pushed Hoddle close to earning the right as one of the All Time Tottenham Greats. Venables, who sold Waddle, said: 'He was one of the best players I have worked with.'

Venables also invested £2 million in Paul Gascoigne in the hope that he might become as influential a figure in a Spurs shirt as Hoddle or indeed Dave Mackay. Venables argues: 'It is

Glenn Hoddle . . . 'born is the king of White Hart Lane'.

a little unfair because it's so difficult for the modern-day players to compare with the former stars as they are only in the middle or at the beginning of their careers, while we are looking back on the careers of the others. Maybe in five years' time the likes of Gazza and Gary Lineker will become candidates to be considered as all-time Tottenham Greats, but they can't possibly be considered at the moment because of the relatively small number of games they've played for the club so far.'

But it remains an unfulfilled ambition of Venables to have worked with Hoddle. He is convinced he would have been able to introduce all the positive elements of Hoddle's game into an effective team pattern.

It is also sad for English football that Hoddle's legacy to the game is still a huge question mark against a player who might not be the best defender in the world but who might just have ignited a brilliant England team.

Hoddle fears that players of exceptional flair are being stifled, killed off by the overriding need for results and robot-type players in the English game.

He believes England are capable of making an impact in World Cups and European Championships — but he is worried that the players of rare talents are not being allowed to play their own game.

'It is a crying shame that we have got the flair players to win things but we don't let them flourish.

'It's like asking a fantastically talented artist, naturally gifted, to be coached to paint in a certain way. He may do a fairly good job, but if he was left free to express himself it would be inspirational.

'We do not allow the free spirit in the international team, not just now but not since Sir Alf Ramsey, it's been the same with Revie and Greenwood.

'Why is it that a player of immense talent like Alan Hudson could win only a couple of caps?

'This type of player is constantly under scrutiny in England. It's a mental block, the way we approach the English game.

'In all honesty the game has stagnated. I've discovered new horizons since playing abroad, experienced different philosophies, and worried that this is not going on back in England.

'Why is it that Ossie Ardiles is the first foreign manager in the English game? Why is it that we seem scared to try new systems?

Exiled superstar relaxing in the paradise playground of Monte Carlo, a long way from the mud and rainy days at Tottenham. His silky skills were more appreciated in France.

'I'm not making a damning indictment of the English game but a damning indictment of the inability to recognise flair and allow it to flourish.

'Yes, it happened to me, but it has happened to others.

'I'm afraid I have to draw the conclusion that we're scared to build a team around an exceptional talent. It's the case not only with Robson, but also his predecessors Revie and Greenwood.

'I think the problem is that people don't understand flair players in England, they don't know how to get the best out of them.

'That goes right through history, I would say until Sir Alf, who knew what he had in Bobby Charlton, and I think he got the best out of him.

'Since then it has been very difficult for a player who has got a different sort of attitude, a different creative attitude to playing football. I always thought that, but it was proved to me by coming abroad. Everyone's mentality and their attitude is different over here. They told me don't do the things you were doing in England, we want to get the best out of you. I don't really think that we understand that in England, everyone has to do a certain job.'

The latest player to suffer the Hoddle syndrome is Paul Gascoigne, and the next could be Southampton's wonder boy Matthew Le Tissier.

Hoddle, in an in-depth radio interview, added: 'I can identify with the talents of Gascoigne, although I can't relate to the personality side because he is a different personality to me.

'It comes back in his face a bit, in the sense when Bobby Robson said he can let you down, I think he means his character, his personality.

'He just doesn't know when to stop, perhaps at the moment, joking and laughing around and when to be a professional, and that is something he has to really knuckle down to.

'If he doesn't do that, then I don't think he's going to be appreciated or taken seriously as a player.

'Professionalism has got to be number one, and then if something else comes along the line and it makes people laugh, that's part of the entertainment side of the game.

'But I don't think Bobby Robson wants to be entertained for 90 minutes. I don't think he wants to sit on the bench laughing. He wants results from Gazza with what he does with the ball.

'The lad has got tremendous talent. He is at a club, working with a manager who will let him express that. The problem is that he is allowed to do certain things at Tottenham that he is not allowed to do when he gets in an England shirt.

'Now does that mean Tottenham are wrong, or does that mean the England manager is wrong?

'It all depends what the manager wants. It depends what Bobby Robson wants from him, and obviously Terry Venables is looking to get the best out of him.

'If you've got somebody with such talent, the object should be to get the best out of him where he will hurt the other team, and that isn't 80 yards from their goal!

Home from a long trip abroad to be welcomed by his attractive wife Anne and two beautiful girls Zoe and Zara.

'You could go on until Doomsday saying Gazza might let you down, until you put him in there and try him a FEW times.

'I think he should have been tried out a little bit more before now.

'I've discovered abroad that these types of players are the first on the team sheet, they are the captains, they are the ones that people admire, the young players are inspired by.

'Whereas in England they still question whether this type of player is good enough. If he is good enough at something creative, it is "but can he do this or that or will he let us down doing his thing?"

'I find it staggering that we still haven't learned in the last 20 years that you have got to encourage and get the best out of the players capable of inspirational football, the players who don't even know how they do it themselves. So how can anyone else read it?'

Hoddle feels as though he has escaped from the shackles of the English system, approach, and preconditioned attitudes, given his freedom to express his delightful talents in France.

He says: 'In England you are continually fighting to be understood. To me it just needed somebody to see what I was good at and get the best out of me.

'Everyone has got different talents. Whether in a company, in business, or in a team, you get the right people to do the right jobs.

'I've no regrets about my many years playing in England, whatsoever. People may say I should have more caps, but I'm happy with the 52, that is an achievement and a half to get that many because of the type of player I am.

'In another country I would have got over 100, but in England there's a lot of players with similar sort of attributes to the game that ended up with one or two caps, or maybe no caps.

'So I am pleased with the 53 I've got, rather than worry about the 50 or 60 that I missed out on.

'I am very proud of my contribution to England. That will always be a great memory to treasure.'

GLENN HODDLE'S PLAYING CAREER

	LEAGUE		F.A. CUP		F.L. CUP		EUROPE		TOTAL	
	App	Gls	App	Gls	App	Gls	App	Gls	App	Gls
1975-76	7	1							7	1
1976-77	39	4	1		2	1			42	5
1977-78	41	12	2	1	2				45	13
1978-79	35	7	7	5	2	1			42	9
1979-80	41	19	6	2	2	1			49	22
1980-81	38	12	9	2	6	1			53	15
1981-82	34	10	7	3	8	1	8	1	57	15
1982-83	24	1	1		3			1	29	1
1983-84	24	4	3		3	1	6		36	5
1984-85	28	8	3			3		6	40	8
1985-86	31	7	5	1	5				41	8
1986-87	36	3	6	1	8	4			50	8
	378	88	50	15	44	10	21	1	491	110

ENGLAND: 1979 v Bulgaria; 1980 v Wales, Australia, Spain; 1981 v Spain, Wales, Scotland, Norway; 1982 v Northern Ireland, Wales, Iceland, Czechoslovakia, Kuwait, Luxembourg; 1983 v Northern Ireland, Scotland, Hungary, Luxembourg; 1984 v France; 1985 v Republic of Ireland, Scotland, Italy, Mexico, West Germany, USA, Rumania, Turkey, Northern Ireland; 1986 v Israel, USSR, Scotland, Mexico, Canada, Portugal, Morocco, Poland, Paraguay, Argentina, Sweden, Northern Ireland, Yugoslavia; 1987 v Spain, Turkey, Scotland; 1988 v West Germany, Turkey, Yugoslavia, Holland, Hungary, Colombia, Eire, Holland, USSR. (53 caps).

CHAPTER 12

Paul Gascoigne

PAUL GASCOIGNE LEFT THESE SHORES A £2 million player before the World Cup — and returned a national hero worth six times that amount.

He illuminated England's world cup campaign with his exciting skills . . . he touched the hearts of millions the moment he broke down in tears after England's brave, bold attempt to reach the Final.

Maggie Thatcher wanted to meet him, the top Italian clubs wanted to buy him.

The whole country went Gazza Crazy.

England finished fourth in the World Cup and Gazza came home with a bronze medal. In a way he has achieved success in reverse, a smash hit with the nation in an England shirt, but still to become successful at club level.

He is loved by Spurs fans, but the season following his World Cup acclaim, Gazza confronts his most searching challenge.

Gazza will fill stadiums wherever he goes, but he will also be a marked man, with defenders out to make their reputations by stopping England's Wonder-boy.

Gazza is on the threshold of joining the elite of Tottenham superstars. He has all the ingredients to break through into the all-time Top Ten of Tottenham Greats. But, for the moment, he is still on the outside looking in.

If he proves to be the inspiration behind a Spurs' championship season, then he will leap into the same category as Glenn Hoddle, Ossie Ardiles, Dave Mackay and Danny Blanchflower.

No doubt Spurs fans are eagerly looking forward to Gazza fulfilling his rich promise.

Gazza has been only two seasons at White Hart Lane, and while he has shown glimpses of his magical ability, Terry Venables will want to see the marked progress in his development continue.

Few young players have made such an impact on English football in so short a space of time, all condensed into those few weeks of World Cup action.

Yet, Gazza would, in all probability, not have made the England starting line-up had Neil Webb steered clear of injury. Webb was first choice alongside skipper Bryan Robson at the start of the World Cup season, only to snap an Achilles tendon on World Cup duty in Sweden.

Gazza went on trial only a couple of months before the World Cup began in the Wembley encounter with the Czechs. An outstanding performance convinced Bobby Robson to test him out against Denmark and Uruguay.

By the end of the World trail, Robson, who once dubbed Gazza 'daft as a brush', hailed him as the most gifted player in his eight-year reign as manager.

Robson nominated Gary Lineker, Bryan Robson, Peter Shilton and Terry Butcher as the outstanding players in his time in charge, but selected Gazza as the best of them all.

Robson's extraordinary tribute was delivered in a passionate World Cup summing up following England's cruel penalty shoot-out defeat by West Germany in Turin.

Robson was a complex mixture of sadness and elation. He had suddenly discovered his best team, and his most startling individual talent . . . just as he was departing for a new career with PSV Eindhoven.

Gazza is the sort of precious talent that had Robson wishing he was staying on as England boss, as he admitted: 'I'm sorry to be losing him.

'But now it is up to the next manager to sort out the most gifted player in the country.'

Robson was asked whether he would like to buy Gazza for the wealthy Dutch club backed by the conglomerate company of Philips. He replied: 'I'd have to sell PSV to buy Gazza.'

Robson's parting shot was to drool over the England jewel of a player who can be the nation's inspiration for the next World Cup assault in the United States in 1994.

'With Gazza it has been short-lived for me,' he said. 'A lot of players I've had have been top-class, but Gazza appears to be on the threshold of something quite unique, something quite different.

'Different from anybody else, that's for sure!

'If he continues on the way he has done, then he is the most cohesive and genuine talent in my eight years as manager.'

Robson spent the entire World Cup campaign praising Gazza for his industry and new-found responsibility. He said: 'He's had six consecutive matches and all have been very good games.

'He has been the best young player in the tournament and he has got a terrific future.

'If he can split the difference between joviality and seriousness, the boy really has got it all. He's had more free-kicks, more corners and gone past more people than anybody else. He's even been chopped down by more people than anybody else.

'But he's still got a little bit to iron out. His release of the ball can be a bit better, a little quicker sometimes. When he keeps getting chopped down he will realise it's best to release the ball earlier.'

On the eve of Gazza and England's finest hour, their semi-final epic against West Germany, coach Don Howe gave a fascinating insight into why the youngster seemed totally uninhibited despite the enormity of the occasion. Howe felt that Gazza simply didn't fully fathom the extent of the big stage in Italy.

It might have been England's biggest match in 24 years but

Fat boy? 'Not me,' says Gazza as he shows off to the fans.

Howe knew Gazza wouldn't freeze. Howe said: 'At first we wondered whether the occasion might affect Gazza but he's never been frightened.

'He hasn't shown any worries about this World Cup. I believe he is just too young to have nerves. When he starts thinking about his football, then he might do.

'When he's older, around 24, or 25, it might suddenly hit him and then he'll worry about the game a bit more. But you don't get nervous at his age. The bigger the occasion, the better he likes it.'

A measure of how rapidly Gazza had grown in stature was that Franz Beckenbauer picked him out, along with Gary Lineker, as the England danger man.

Beckenbauer argued that England had not suffered as much as everyone though they might with the loss of their injured skipper Bryan Robson — and to a large extent that was due to the effectiveness of Gazza.

The man who ulimately triumphed in Italy said: 'The loss of skipper Bryan Robson is no longer such a tragedy for Bobby Robson and that is because Gascoigne has taken over his role and become the major influence on the side. He can lift the team like Robson used to do so frequently. The fact is he has become on of the big players in the torunament and he has also become so important to England.'

Beckenbauer even made the extravagant suggestion that Gazza could have won the World Cup for England, the way he played against the Germans perhaps he might have done.

But the yellow card in the semi-final meant that Gazza would not have been eligible for the Final. Bobby Charlton said that if there was one consolation for England not reaching the Final it was that Gazza would not have suffered the terrible anguish of missing out. Not only that, but England's chances of lifting the biggest soccer prize of all would have been severely damaged by the absence of their most influential player.

Mark Wright and Des Walker also enjoyed marvellous World Cups, but Gazza was the most successful of all England's creative players, and few would have guessed that would be likely prior to the competition.

Jimmy Greaves had no hesitation in nominating Gazza his 'Man of the World Cup '90'.

He said: 'I put him up there with Lother Matthaeus and Toto Schillaci as the player of the tournament and ahead of

Trouble-shooter! Gazza is clearly shooting to the top in soccer.

them because of the richness of his promise. There is more to come. He has been a razzler-dazzler throughout the Finals and he can hold his head highest of all England's heroes.

'If his double booking had cost him a place in that Final it would have been like exhibiting the crown jewels without the biggest diamond.

'There was one Englishman in the Turin stadium who can have felt happy when all thw shooting and the shouting was over after one of the finest World Cup semi-finals of all time.

'Graham Taylor, England's next manager, knew even in the moment of our heartbreak that Bobby Robson has left him a fantastic foundation on which to build England's 1994 World Cup challenge.

Yet Gazza went into the finals as an enigma. Could he

control his temperament? Did he have the stamina? Would he be willing to work when it was sweat rather than skill that was needed?

'He passed every test with honours and is now the mature, finished article — a gold-plated superstar of the game who is going to put thousands on the gates wherever he performs with Tottenham next season.

'I lumbered Gascoigne with the nickname "Fat Boy" back in his days at Newcastle when he stuffed his mouth as hungrily as he stuffed the opposition. The Goliath from Gateshead was in danger of weighing himself down with carbohydrates instead of medals.

'Terry Venables must take a lot of the credit for getting discipline harnessed to his daring and genius.

'Gazza is now almost slimline, and during the World Cup he has produced some of the most devastating midfield performances I've seen from an England player since Duncan Edwards. What I love about Gazza is his obvious passion for the game. He wears his heart on his sleeve and he gets us all sharing his joy and heartbreak.

'All I hope is nobody ever tries to knock the sparkling individuality out of his play. It's his personality that makes him the player he is.'

Few are closer to Gazza in footballing terms than his Tottenham team-mate Gary Lineker. He has witnessed all his trials and tribulations in his early days at White Hart Lane trying to justify what was a huge fee at the time, and attempting to come to terms with a vastly new and different environment to the North East.

Lineker believes he spotted the exact moment when Gazza was transformed from a boy to a man.

'For me, the worst moment of young Gazza's life in football was the real making of him. The terrible moment when he knew a second yellow card had put him out of the World Cup Final he was trying so hard to reach with England.

'That's when he grew up. That's when he showed me what he was made of. I don't mind admitting I was worried about

It ain't half hot, mum! Gazza displays all his skills under a scorching sun.

him. I'd seen the look on his face and he was totally
devastated. I even ran over to our bench to tell them to keep an
eye on him. He might have turned aggressive, he might have
disappeared from the game, he might have lost team discipline.
Anything was possible.'

For a few moments Gazza visibly wobbled. The tears welled up in his eyes. His first thought was that he had let down the team and the manager who had persistently warned him against any rash tackles, that his responsibility was to the team. A few seconds later the devastating realisation that he had been banned from the World Cup Final set in. Little wonder that his mind began to wander from the match.

Lineker went on: 'I asked Gazza if he was alright and said: "Listen, you've been brilliant, but we need you to keep going for us."

'It was asking a lot of a 23-year-old who is such an England fan that, if he wasn't playing for us, he'd be on the terraces singing his heart out.

'Gazza just nodded and started demanding the ball more than ever. He was as good as anyone toward the end of the match.

'You couldn't devise a more searching test for a highly-strung character who is always on edge. And I'll never forget the way he passed it.'

Veteran of the 1986 World Cup campaign where he finished with the Golden Boot as top scorer, Lineker doesn't underestimate the extent of Gazza's influence in Italy on the England team.

'I'll never forget the part he played when Bryan Robson had to go off in the match against Holland. Gazza took on Bryan's role, encouraging everybody to keep giving everything.

'I had seen him do that for Spurs at times, but his problem was he'd get carried away and start moaning. It's often the way with very talented performers who find it hard to accept that others haven't got the same gifts.

'But he's getting on top of that now. It doesn't worry me because I just ignored him when he had a go for Spurs. World football, though, can't ignore him now. Where he was once known for his pranks, he is now known for his football.'

Greaves demands that the game encourage characters, but it is vital that football comes first and the clowning is reserved for the appropriate time only. But Greaves doesn't want to change Gazza.

Greaves says: 'If you wonder where he gets his sense of humour from, just listen to this quote from his dad moments after the semi-final. The question put to Gazza senior by a reporter in Gateshead was: "What do you think Paul is going through now?" Dad, wiping back a tear, said: "The shower. He'll be going through the shower."

'With lines like that can you wonder that his son Gazza is a one-off. And we love every inch of him.'

The England camp resounds with stories about Gazza's cheek, mischief, and general sense of fun.

When Robson called him daft as a brush he came out for training the next morning with a lavatory brush stuck down the side of his socks.

When the England team arrived in Bolgna for the match against Belgium, the England manager discovered Gazza playing tennis with an American tourist in the middle of the afternoon. Robson was livid. The England manager ordered his player off the tennis court and simply explained that Gazza cannot sit still for a moment.

He has got himself into several off-the-field scraps, but there is another side to Gazza. He gave away his England shirt that he wore against Czechoslovakia to his godson William Roeder, and throughout the World Cup kept in touch by telephone. His close pal, Watford captain Glen Roeder — a former Newcastle United team-mate — recalls: 'It just sums up Paul. He is a very ordinary, caring lad and isn't interested in being regarded as a superstar.

'We're close mates but he wasn't just ringing to speak to me. He also takes his respopnsiiblities as godfather seriously and wanted to talk to William. His phone bill must have looked like a king's ransom. I kept thinking of what it was costing him but he never wanted to end the conversation. Despite everything going on in Italy, he was interested in what we were doing and what the news was over here.'

Gazza must have done an awful lot of talking as baby William's only words were 'hello — Gazza!'

Gazza was born on May 27, 1967 in one room rented in a terraced riverside house in Pitt Street, Gateshead, Tyne and Wear. He weighed in at 7½lb. His parents were poor and the room, with just a bed and a wardrobe, was all they could afford. It was so impoverished, a false leg even fell out of the wardrobe when they moved in!

His mother recalls: 'As soon as he could stand, he was kicking a football.'

He would drive his parents to distraction at meal times by juggling a football under the dinner table. Carol adds: 'He ended with tea all over him. As I mopped up he would say, "I'm sorry mam, but I'm getting better at football".'

At four he walked up to his dad John and said: 'Can I have a football for my birthday and Christmas please? I want to play for England, daddy. I'm going to be a best player.'

At six he would go to the shop next door at their new two-bedroomed council home in the Dunston area for his mother but was always dribbling a football.

At eight John lied about Paul's age to enrol him as a member of Redheugh Boy's Club, two years early because they had a good team.

At ten he had won his first football trophy — for penalty kicks in a competition in the North East. Carol says: 'He took it to bed and kept it under his pillow.'

At 14 he was signed up as a schoolboy player for his favourite club, Newcastle United.

Once when Gazza was juggling a football indoors he knocked the water jug crashing onto the floor. He said cheekily: 'Argh, dad, it's only a jug — just you wait and see, I'll get you a better one when I play for England!'

He did a lot better than that. When he signed for Spurs as a £2 million player, he acquired a £250,000 home in Hertfordshire, a new black Mercedes . . . and he bought his parents a £100,000 bungalow in Dunston.

Proud father John said: 'My lad just knew he was going to be the best footballer ever. I remember when we bought him

The Breast of British! Gazza during England's triumphant return after the World Cup in Italy.

that first ball. It was only a few shillings. But from the day we put the ball in his hand, he was never without it. He was always saying, ''Just you wait, I'm going to be the best ever.''

'When he was five, he got his first pair of boots, they were so small, I could fit them in the palm of my hand. But he was so proud that he wore them allthe time, and when they weren't on his feet, he would be sitting there on the kitchen floor, cleaning them like they were the crown jewels.'

Geoff Wilson, who ran the under-15 team at Heathfield High School in Gateshead, remembers the young Gascoigne.

'He had a round face, round body and round legs. But I've never seen so much skill in a young player — it was amazing.'

Gazza graduated through the representative ranks of both Gateshead and Durham Boys but League clubs were not exactly falling over themselves to sign him.

Ironically Bobby Robson was among those club managers who rejected Gascoigne. Ipswich Town, Middlesbrough and Southampton all turned their backs on him before Newcastle took a chance. I wonder how they are feeling now?

Willie McFaul had seen Gazza play for his school but it was youth development officer Peter Kirkley, who had shown such faith in Peter Beardsley, who was convinced the lad had a future in the professional game.

'He was small and chubby and a bit of a plodder,' recalls Kirkley. 'But he had exceptional skill. There was something about him that made you feel good.'

In his early days Gazza was hooked on Mars bars, ice creams, cans of pop, mince pies and everything sweet. He was so overweight, there was a danger he would be thrown out of the club.

He admits: 'I would sit in front of the TV gorging myself silly. I thought it would be okay because I'd be able to burn off the extra calories. But I became podgy.'

Jack Charlton, Newcastle boss at the time, called Gazza into his office.

Big Jack told him bluntly: 'Get that excess weight off in a fortnight or you're out on your ear.' Gazza was scared of Big Jack and his booming orders and lost half a stone in a week. His career was saved.

Gazza was an apprentice in the Kevin Keegan era at St. James's Park, and quite naturally, like so many kids, revered the former England skipper. He was assigned to clean Keegan's boots and one day Keegan gave him three pairs of boots to break in, wearing them around the house . . . but Gazza lost one of them on the way home.

'I was on the Metro showing Keegan's boots to some of

Goal! Gazza on England Under-21 duty.

my mates. But when I got him I discovered one was missing. I panicked. I went back to the Metro, looking round all the stations, and I searched the bus I'd also travelled on. But I couldn't find the boot anywhere. I thought I'd be sacked. I was in a blind panic and chickened out, asking my dad to tell Kevin what had happened. But Kevin was great — he just shrugged and said he hadn't liked the boots anyway.'

During Charlton's one-year reign as manager Gazza was the inspiration behind Newcastle United's F.A. Youth Cup triumph, the juniors equivalent to the F.A. Cup. Gazza was the skipper who scored twice in the 4-1 away leg victory at

Watford. Elton John came into the dressing room to offer his congratulations and the lads were naturally a little nervous. Not Gazza. He piped up from the back: 'Give us a song, Elton!'

Gazza made a couple of First Division appearanced under Big Jack as a sub but his full League debut came in Willie McFaul's first match as manager at Southampton at the beginning of season 1985-86. United drew.

It was a season when Beardsley was the No. 1 star. How ironic that in the 1990 World Cup Finals Gazza totally eclipsed Beardsley.

Paul Goddard once gripped Gazza by the throat when he tried to over-elaborate and score a wonder goal when he had done all the hard work with his brilliant skills. Then Mirandinha arrived from South America, the first Brazilian to play in the Football League. There didn't seem room in the same team for two players of such immense individuality.

Two individuals with such a high belief in themselves argued like crazy on the field. Each believed the other wouldn't pass him the salt never mind the ball. It was seen by the crowd, it made headline news, and it created a major talking point on Tyneside.

Gazza can crack jokes, play the showman on the pitch, but there is also a sensitive side to his nature.

He felt at home entertaining live audiences with his sharp wit in Newcastle clubs, but when one of the fans wondered why he wouldn't re-sign for Newcastle at £2,000-a-week when an ordinary fan spends his hard-earned cash to watch him, he was deeply hurt. He went missing from the post talk-in hospitality room and was found sobbing in the toilets.

He suffered enormous criticism about his off-the-field behaviour when he arrived at Spurs. Again he was badly affected.

While Gazza was the clown prince of English soccer, Bobby Robson couldn't be sure whether he could be trusted. The World Cup ended all such doubts. The World Cup placed Gazza in a sphere that he never dreamed was possible.

Even mega-rich Juventus President Gianni Agnelli was taken aback by Gazza's World Cup contribution. Agnelli, whose family own car giant Fiat, said: 'Gascoigne is a dog of war with a face like a child.'

Gazza was Agnellis favourite player of the tournament, and that meant that every Italian club would want the Spurs star, with Juventus sure to head the queue. There is a saying in Italy — if Agnelli wants something he gets it.

But Gazza likes nothing better than to get out onto the river bank and relax by fishing with his favourite rod and line. 'Fishing helps keep me sane,' he confesses.

'I didn't come into football to get rich quick. I don't want to be a millionaire, just one of the best players in the world and I can get that for free.

'I know I could easily earn more by agreeing to do extra personal appearances or take on more contracts but that's not for me.

'Playing football is my whole life and after that it's all about relaxation and going fishing.

'I'm not bothered about nightclubs any more. I don't want to be someone who loves being noticed in this club or that. I would rather be recognised out on the pitch. I don't even get involved in any money deals. I leave all that to my business manager. He knows that there is much more cash to be had through my football, but he has never pushed me and agreed with my attitude.

'I was introduced to fishing three years ago and since then that's what you will find me doing on many of my spare days. It's the best therapy of the lot. Taking up fishing was the best thing I ever did.

'When the criticism was at its height — when the back stabbers were really landing the vicious blows — I was thankful that I had my fishing as my release from al the pressures.'

But Gazza is going to find the commercial pressures increasing. Almost overnight in Italy he has become English soccer's most marketable product.

His business advisers quickly spotted the potential and quickly registered the name of 'Gazza' as a trademark with manufacturers clamouring for him to endorse their products.

His accountant Lennard Lazarus said: 'Nobody can now use the name "Gazza" without a licence from his company, Paul Gascoigne Promotions.

'We have also registered Gascoigne's signature. He is the only person the general public knows as Gazza, and we are protecting that name so he can decide how it should be used for commercial purposes and which products he wants to be associated with. Put smply, his company owns the right to the use of that name, just as if it were Dick Tracy or Mickey Mouse.

'We are looking at many proposals — phone calls are coming in by the minute — and there are deals in negotiation.' Before the World Cup Gazza marketed a computer game, and a Christmas book under his name but Italy magnified his earning capability. That was highlighted during England's homecoming parade when women fans sported 'We Love You Gazza' T-shirts.

The Gazza Factor was quoted as the reason behind an 8p leap in Spurs shares. Even the Stock Exchange was impressed by his footballing genius in the World Cup, and Spurs were sure that would be reflected in increased gates.

'Gazza will become the next Bobby Charlton in the nation's affection,' commented the Spurs chairman Irving Scholar in the *Sunday Times*.

It was Scholar who sanctioned the £2 million record fee to bring Gazza to Spurs, a move not universally accepted. Terry Venables wanted the player and Scholar made the money available.

Scholar's conversion began on a January afternoon in 1988, when he was sitting next to Venables at St. James's Park as Spurs were struggling against Newcastle, largely because Gazza, Newcastle's 20-year-old midfield player, was in control of the game. Gazza scored twice as Spurs lost 2-0 and both

One man and his dog. Gazza meets an old friend back home on Tyneside.

of the game. Gazza scored twice as Spurs lost 2-0 and both Venables and Scholar knew that a new Geordie talent, better than Beardsley, better than Waddle, had emerged.

Five months later Gazza signed for Spurs for £2 million, a week after his 21st birthday.

'Some people though I was mad,' Venables recalls. 'I got tremendous stick in the mail. But I couldn't see how he was going to be a risk. At first he was fat — you forget how fat he was. He had to lose a stone and a half. He did it himself, dieting and training, but then he didn't have the strength to run.'

With Spurs' opening game of the season against Coventry

called off because of incomplete ground work, Gazza's Tottenham debut was at Newcastle. The Geordie fans jeered him, threw Mars bars, and Gazza came off with cramp.

But his home debut was against Arsenal, and although Spurs lost 3-2 to the old enemy Gazza scored, in his socks, after his boot came off.

After a year Venables was convinced about the conversion of Gazza from a clown to a clown prince of English soccer, but Bobby Robson took more time to accept it.

Now, the player who is so patriotic he wears Union Jack underpants, has become as synonymous with the Bulldog spirit of English football as Bobby Charlton.

Gazza is determined that the World Cup won't change him.

He says: 'The proudest thing I have ever done in my life was taking my World Cup medal round the four schools I went to the week I returned from Italy. No-one asked me to do it. I just wanted to share what I felt with the kids who were like me.'

He celebrated his return from Italy with a few pints at Dunston Excelsior Working Men's Club, where his dad first took him when was about nine and sat him in the corner with a Coke and packet of crisps.

His dad had arranged a homecoming that was something special. The Club was packed out, and when Gazza came into the room, the noise was deafening.

Gazza says: 'It's the one place I come in, shut the doors, chalk my name up on the snooker board, and just be me. Just the same as everyone else.

'I don't really model myself on anybody. I have no ambitions to be like anyone else. I used to clean Kevin Keegan's boots. He was the first big football star I ever came into close contact with. He was great to me and I admired him very much as a player and for what he did for Newcastle.'

Because of his fierce desire to stay one of the lads, he found himself surreptitiously peeling a £10 note from the wad

wad in his pocket when he was out with his mates at a pizza restaurant. 'I didn't want to suddenly produce a pile of money in front of them. It would have made them uncomfortable and me, too.'

Equally as he drove his Merc around Newcastle and Gateshead, he was ill at ease when making a call on his car phone. He rapped out the number with the phone on his knees. 'It might be alright in London, but I don't want to be seen as the flash bastard here.'

Gazza has got a taste for champagne and the good life, but back home in the North East is where he feels most relaxed.

'I like to drink champagne if I'm out socially. It's best for my weight. But normally I wouldn't drink it when I'm out with the lads but if they ask my to buy champagne, then I'll do it because it gives me a kick to see them enjoying it as well.

'The most important thing in my life is the people I grew up with. I couldn't care a stuff what anyone else thinks. But I would hate the people here to think less of me. I'm going to protect that, I swear.

'If you come back here in five year's time, I'll still be the same Gazza.'

PAUL GASCOIGNE'S PLAYING CAREER AT TOTTENHAM

	LEAGUE		F.A. CUP		F.L. CUP		EUROPE		TOTAL	
	App	Gls	App	Gls	App	Gls	App	Gls	App	Gls
1988-89	32	6	5	1					37	7
1989-90	34	6	4	1					38	7
	66	12	9	2					75	14

ENGLAND: 1988 v Denmark, Saudi Arabia; 1989 v Albania, Chile, Scotland, Sweden; 1990 v Brazil, Czechoslovakia, Denmark, Uruguay, Tunisia, Republic of Ireland, Holland, Egypt, Belgium, Cameroon, West Germany (17 caps).

CHAPTER 13

Bill Nicholson

BILL NICHOLSON IS ONE OF ONLY FOUR MEN who have won the Championship as a player and a manager with the same club, Kenny Dalglish, Howard Kendall and George Graham being the others.

Nicholson was an outstanding wing-half for Spurs in the brilliant and gifted '50s push-and-run side under manager Arthur Rowe. At most clubs Nicholson's talents as a player would qualify him for the privilege of inclusion in the all-time great players.

He doesn't quite make it as a player, but that's only because of the extraordinary depth of talents through the years of high-quality international stars who have turned out for the Spurs.

But there is no dispute, absolutely none, that he makes the grade as Tottenham's All-Time Great Manager.

Bill Nicholson is to Spurs what Bill Shankly is to Liverpool.

Nicholson, manager of Spurs for 16 years, led the club to the Double, the first club to win the coveted, seemingly unattainable, F.A. Cup and First Division Championship this century.

Ian St. John has no doubt that Shankly was the all-time master-manager of Anfield, George Graham would nominate Herbert Chapman as the manager supreme for the Gunners, and there is no question that Sir Matt Busby is the king of Old Trafford. Terry Venables, without hesitation, nominates Bill Nicholson in the same league. So no book about the Greats of

The art of full-back play. Bill Nicholson demonstrates the correct method of execution of a sliding tackle back in 1946.

Tottenham Hotspur would be complete without reference to the managerial genius of Bill Nicholson.

Nicholson came close to creating the perfect team — the Double side of 1961. Debates have raged for years whether that team was better than the sides created by Herbert Chapman at Arsenal, Sir Matt Busby at Manchester United or by Bill Shankly at Liverpool.

Many would argue that Nicholson forged the best of them all, captained by Danny Blanchflower, with players of the supreme multi-talents of Dave Mackay, Cliff Jones, and Bobby Smith, and in the next season supplemented by Jimmy Greaves.

That team summed up everything good about the beautiful game.

Nicholson, himself, was a man whose hallmarks were honesty, hard work, and perfection. He relentlessly, remorselessly sought the perfect team, and many will argue that he found it. He often presented a gruff, unco-operative exterior to the outside world, but his motive was to keep everything away from his beloved team.

But that was not the real Nicholson. I have been in a privileged position to have captured a glimpse of the real Nicholson.

When I first joined the *North London Weekly Herald* as a raw sports reporter, one of my first tasks, as successor to David Leggett, was to be appointed as the 'Spurs Man' . . . to report and cover all the Spurs matches home and away with one entire page in the broadsheet weekly paper devoted to the club.

Leggett took me to White Hart Lane by appointment to meet Mr Bill Nicholson, the Tottenham Hotspur manager at that time, the greatest manager in the club's history.

After a short wait we were ushered into his office at the back of the 'house' that fronted the old West Stand.

For a lifelong Spurs fan, such a meeting was a privilege and a thrill. I was very nervous. But the manager put me at ease and asked what I would require from him, as a working professional relationship. He seemed very friendly, nothing like the kind of man who had been described to me, that is, someone who detested the Press and had very little to do with them, and who co-operated very little. Encouraged by his responsive attitude I said: 'I'd like to see you once a week, perhaps every Monday.' He looked at me surprised. 'Well, we shall have to see about that,' he said. 'Let's give it a try to start with, come and see me on Monday morning.'

When I left the office, Leggett, who had been doing the job for quite a few years, said: 'Bill Nicholson saw me once a season, not once a week!'

But I saw him once a week for the next four years.

One day I was late. Not too late, but about ten to fifteen minutes. I had always been punctual in the past, and he struck me as a man who was punctual himself. 'I'm really sorry, I'm late,' I pleaded, 'but my watch had stopped.' It was a pretty feeble excuse but it was the truth. He looked at me for a minute, and thought for another minute. I'm sure he believed

For the purpose of demonstration Bill Nicholson illustrates the wrong way to deliver a sliding tackle.

my lame excuse to be an honest one, at least. He reached down and opened one of the drawers behind his desk. 'Here', he said, 'you've no excuse for being late, have you?' He handed me a watch, an AC Milan watch that had been given to him during one of Spurs' European Cup ties.

Nicholson became Spurs manager in October 1958 and began his new career with a 10-4 victory over Everton.

He recalls how Jimmy Anderson celebrated fifty years as an employee of the club but called him into his office at a time when everyone expected him to quit as manager. Nicholson says: 'He called me into his office and told me that Fred Wale, the vice-chairman, wanted to see me at his works, Brown's of Tottenham.

'What's it all about, Jim?' I asked.

'You go down there,' he said. 'You'll soon find out.'

I drove to Mr Wale's premises and he welcomed me into his office.

Heading down to feet. This is the 'wrong' way — another aspect of full-back play demonstrated by Bill Nicholson at White Hart Lane in 1946.

'Jimmy Anderson isn't going to carry on as manager,' he said. 'Would you like the job?'

'There was no suggestion at the time that Anderson was ill, but when the announcement was made three days later, on the morning of a home match against Everton, it was said he had retired though ill health.

'Mr Wale made no mention of a pay increase or a contract, and I didn't raise the subject either. I never had a contract in my life as a manager. I reasoned that if I was good enough to do the job they would keep me. If I wasn't good

Bill Nicholson parades the Football League Cup at the club's training ground at Cheshunt in August 1973.

enough to do it, they would sack me. A contract wouldn't make any difference. I told Mr Wale I would like to do the job. I had been coaching at the club for four years and felt I could do it.

'Fine,' he said.

Spurs were 16th in the table with nine points from their first 11 games. Everton were in the bottom three. Spurs won 10-4 with Tommy Harmer making most of the goals and Bobby Smith scoring four. The total of 14 goals equalled a First Division record set when Aston Villa had beaten Accrington 12-2 sixty-six years earlier.

Within two years Spurs had won the Double, and when Danny Blanchflower collected the F.A. Cup to complete a feat that was thought to be impossible at the time Nicholson recalls: 'I was not too excited. If I won £1 million on the pools or in a newspaper competition, I wouldn't jump for joy. If something has been your ambition and you've achieved it, then that's fine. If anything, I felt a sense of slight dissatisfaction. I had wanted to play well and show how good we were, but the Final had not been particularly entertaining. I wasn't conscious of being caught up in any euphoria. Some of the players felt the same way. In those days you weren't mobbed by television reporters or the Press. There were no Press conferences or countless interviews with radio reporters. I don't remember giving a Press conference, although I did speak informally to some reporters afterwards.

'I don't recall being over-elated, either, at the banquet after our victory. I looked on our success as an honour that meant more to the club than to any individual. At the time I was earning little — around £1,500, which was about twice the national average but no more than the top players — though I did receive a small bonus later as an acknowledgement of my work. I suspect it fell a long way short of the bonuses being paid to managers these days!'

Honesty was Nicholson's trademark. He is a simple man of simple tastes, a Yorkshireman, who moved to within walking distance of the ground and never switched to a more luxurious house even when he was manager. He wanted to be as close as possible to his work. Often when I would be working late, I would pass his office and the light would still be burning. In today's game, managers often follow their players home after training. Nicholson was at his desk for long hours, or scouring the country for new players, or watching opposition teams. He devoted his life to Spurs.

After he was unceremoniously shown the door by a wretched Spurs board, he went to West Ham, returning once Irving Scholar took control of the club. It was Irving Scholar who approached me with the idea of writing Bill Nicholson's autobiography. At first Bill declined point blank to write his autobiography. 'I was made very lucrative offers as soon as I resigned as Spurs manager, I even had one journalist turn up on my doorstep making offers. But I never intended to either cash in on what happened at Spurs, or bother with making any revelations that might upset anybody because I knew I would have to tell the truth. My satisfaction came from what I achieved.'

Manager and captain of the famous 'Double' team at a recent reunion in London.

I persuaded Bill that he owed it to all his followers, owed it to the history of the club, to explain the inside story of the most successful manager in the history of Spurs. He agreed under my intense pressure. And I thank him for and on behalf of all Spurs fans for that decision. I also thank Irving Scholar for the idea in the first place. It was a privilege to collaborate with my one-time colleague on the *Daily Mail*, Brian Scovell, in compiling the book *Glory, Glory, My Life With Spurs*.

Nicholson has devoted more than 50 years of his life and very soul to Spurs, and his bust adorns the entrance to Spurs' impressive £5 million West Stand, like the bust of Herbert Chapman in the Marble Halls of Highbury. No one deserves such lavish recognition more than Bill Nicholson.

BILL NICHOLSON'S PLAYING CAREER

	LEAGUE		F.A. CUP		F.L. CUP		EUROPE		TOTAL	
	App	Gls	App	Gls	App	Gls	App	Gls	App	Gls
1938-39	8								8	
1946-47	39		2						41	
1947-48	38		5						43	
1948-49	42	2	1						43	2
1949-50	39	2	3						42	2
1950-51	41	1	1						42	1
1951-52	37	1	2						39	1
1952-53	31		7						38	
1953-54	30		6						36	
1954-55	10								10	
	315	6	27						342	6

ENGLAND: 1951 v Portugal (1 cap).

Tottenham Hotspur Honours

Football League Division One
Champions: 1951, 1961
Runners-up: 1922, 1952, 1957, 1963

Football League Division Two
Champions: 1920, 1950
Runners-up: 1909, 1933

F.A. Cup
Winners: 1901, 1921, 1961, 1962, 1967, 1981, 1982
Runners-up: 1987

Football League Cup
Winners: 1971, 1973
Runners-up: 1982

European Cup Winners' Cup
Winners: 1963
Runners-up: 1982

UEFA Cup
Winners: 1972, 1984
Runners-up: 1974

Tottenham Hotspur Facts

Season	P	W	D	L	F	A	Pts	Position
DIVISION TWO								
1930-31	42	22	7	13	88	55	51	3rd
1931-32	42	16	11	15	87	78	43	8th
1932-33	42	20	15	7	96	51	55	2nd
DIVISION ONE								
1933-34	42	21	7	14	79	56	49	3rd
1934-35	42	10	10	22	54	93	30	22nd
DIVISION TWO								
1935-36	42	18	13	11	91	55	49	5th
1936-37	42	17	9	16	88	66	43	10th
1937-38	42	19	6	17	76	54	44	5th
1938-39	42	19	9	14	67	62	47	8th
1946-47	42	17	14	11	65	53	48	6th
1947-48	42	15	14	13	56	43	44	8th
1948-49	42	17	16	9	72	44	50	5th
1949-50	42	27	7	8	81	35	61	1st
DIVISION ONE								
1950-51	42	25	10	7	82	44	60	1st
1951-52	42	22	9	11	76	51	53	2nd
1952-53	42	15	11	16	78	69	41	10th
1953-54	42	16	5	21	65	76	37	16th
1954-55	42	16	8	18	72	73	40	16th
1955-56	42	15	7	20	61	71	37	18th
1956-57	42	22	12	8	104	56	56	2nd
1957-58	42	21	9	12	93	77	51	3rd
1958-59	42	13	10	19	85	95	36	18th

Season	P	W	D	L	F	A	Pts	Position
				DIVISION ONE				
1959-60	42	21	11	10	86	50	53	3rd
1960-61	42	31	4	7	115	55	66	1st
1961-62	42	21	10	11	88	69	52	3rd
1962-63	42	23	9	10	111	62	55	2nd
1963-64	42	22	7	13	97	81	51	4th
1964-65	42	19	7	16	87	71	45	6th
1965-66	42	16	12	14	75	66	44	8th
1966-67	42	24	8	10	71	48	56	3rd
1967-68	42	19	9	14	70	59	47	7th
1968-69	42	14	17	11	61	51	45	6th
1969-70	42	17	9	16	54	55	43	11th
1970-71	42	19	14	9	54	33	52	3rd
1971-72	42	19	13	10	63	42	51	6th
1972-73	42	16	13	13	58	48	45	8th
1973-74	42	14	14	14	45	50	42	11th
1974-75	42	13	8	21	52	63	34	19th
1975-76	42	14	15	13	63	63	43	9th
1976-77	42	12	9	21	48	72	33	22nd
				DIVISION TWO				
1977-78	42	20	16	6	83	49	56	3rd
				DIVISION ONE				
1978-79	42	13	15	14	48	61	41	11th
1979-80	42	15	10	17	52	62	40	14th
1980-81	42	14	15	13	70	68	43	10th
1981-82	42	20	11	11	67	48	71	4th
1982-83	42	20	9	13	65	50	69	4th
1983-84	42	17	10	15	44	65	61	8th
1984-85	42	23	8	11	78	51	77	3rd
1985-86	42	19	8	15	74	52	65	10th
1986-87	42	21	8	13	68	43	71	3rd
1987-88	40	12	11	17	38	48	47	13th
1988-89	38	15	12	11	60	46	57	6th
1989-90	38	19	6	13	59	47	63	3rd

Tottenham's F.A. Cup Record

1930-31

Round 3	Preston North End	(h)	3-1
Round 4	W.B.A.	(a)	0-1

1931-32

Round 3	Sheffield Wednesday	(h)	2-2
Round 3 (R)	Sheffield Wednesday	(a)	1-3

1932-33

Round 3	Oldham Athletic	(a)	6-0
Round 4	Luton Town	(a)	0-2

1933-34

Round 3	Everton	(h)	3-0
Round 4	West Ham United	(h)	4-1
Round 5	Aston Villa	(h)	0-1

1934-35

Round 3	Manchester City	(h)	1-0
Round 4	Newcastle United	(h)	2-0
Round 5	Bolton Wanderers	(h)	1-1
Round 5 (R)	Bolton Wanderers	(a)	1-1
Round 5 (R)	Bolton Wanderers	Villa Park	0-2

1935-36

Round 3	Southend United	(h)	4-4
Round 3 (R)	Southend United	(a)	2-1
Round 4	Huddersfield Town	(h)	1-0
Round 5	Bradford City	(a)	0-0
Round 5 (R)	Bradford City	(h)	2-1
Round 6	Sheffield United	(a)	1-3

1936-37

Round 3	Portsmouth	(a)	5-0
Round 4	Plymouth Argyle	(h)	1-0
Round 5	Everton	(a)	1-1
Round 5 (R)	Everton	(h)	4-3
Round 6	Preston North End	(h)	1-3

1937-38

Round 3	Blackburn Rovers	(h)	3-2
Round 4	New Brighton	(a)	0-0
Round 4 (R)	New Brighton	(h)	5-2
Round 5	Chesterfield	(a)	2-2
Round 5 (R)	Chesterfield	(h)	2-1
Round 6	Sunderland	(h)	0-1

1938-39

Round 3	Watford	(h)	7-1
Round 4	West Ham United	(a)	3-3
Round 4 (R)	West Ham United	(h)	1-1 (after extra time)
Round 4 (R)	West Ham United	Highbury	1-2

1945-46

Round 3	Brentford	(h)	2-2
Round 3 (R)	Brentford	(a)	0-2

1946-47

Round 3	Stoke City	(h)	2-2
Round 3 (R)	Stoke City	(a)	0-1

1947-48

Round 3	Bolton Wanderers	(a)	2-0 (after extra time)
Round 4	W.B.A.	(h)	3-1
Round 5	Leicester City	(h)	5-2
Round 6	Southampton	(a)	1-0
Semi Final	Blackpool	Villa Park	1-3 (after extra time)

1948-49

Round 3	Arsenal	(a)	0-3

1949-50

Round 3	Stoke City	(a)	1-0
Round 4	Sunderland	(h)	5-1
Round 5	Everton	(a)	0-1

1950-51

Round 3	Huddersfield Town	(a)	0-2

1951-52

Round 3	Scunthorpe	(a)	3-0
Round 4	Newcastle United	(h)	0-3

1952-53

Round 3	Tranmere Rovers	(a)	1-1
Round 3 (R)	Tranmere Rovers	(h)	9-1
Round 4	Preston North End	(a)	2-2
Round 4 (R)	Preston North End	(h)	1-0
Round 5	Halifax Town	(a)	3-0
Round 6	Birmingham City	(a)	1-1
Round 6 (R)	Birmingham City	(h)	2-2 (after extra time)
Round 6 (R)	Birmingham City	Molineux	1-0
Semi Final	Blackpool	Villa Park	1-2

1953-54

Round 3	Leeds United	(a)	3-3
Round 3 (R)	Leeds United	(h)	1-0
Round 4	Manchester City	(a)	1-0
Round 5	Hull City	(a)	1-1
Round 5 (R)	Hull City	(h)	2-0
Round 6	W.B.A.	(a)	0-3

1954-55

Round 3	Gateshead	(a)	2-0
Round 4	Port Vale	(h)	4-2
Round 5	York City	(a)	1-3

1955-56

Round 3	Boston United	(h)	4-0
Round 4	Middlesbrough	(h)	3-1
Round 5	Doncaster	(a)	2-0
Round 6	West Ham United	(h)	3-3
Round 6 (R)	West Ham United	(a)	2-1
Semi Final	Manchester City	Villa Park	0-1

1956-57

Round 3	Leicester City	(h)	2-0
Round 4	Chelsea	(h)	4-0
Round 5	Bournemouth	(a)	1-3

1957-58

| Round 3 | Leicester City | (h) | 4-0 |
| Round 4 | Sheffield United | (h) | 0-3 |

1958-59

Round 3	West Ham United	(h)	2-0
Round 4	Newport County	(h)	4-1
Round 5	Norwich City	(h)	1-1
Round 5 (R)	Norwich City	(a)	0-1

1959-60

Round 3	Newport County	(a)	4-0
Round 4	Crewe Alexandra	(a)	2-2
Round 4 (R)	Crewe Alexandra	(h)	13-2
Round 5	Blackburn Rovers	(h)	1-3

1960-61

Round 3	Charlton Athletic	(h)	3-2
Round 4	Crewe Alexandra	(h)	5-1
Round 5	Aston Villa	(a)	2-0
Round 6	Sunderland	(a)	1-1
Round 6 (R)	Sunderland	(h)	5-0
Semi Final	Burnley	Villa Park	3-0
Final	Leicester City	Wembley	2-0

1961-62

Round 3	Birmingham City	(a)	3-3
Round 3 (R)	Birmingham City	(h)	4-2
Round 4	Plymouth Argyle	(a)	5-1
Round 5	W.B.A.	(a)	4-2
Round 6	Aston Villa	(h)	2-0
Semi Final	Manchester United	Hillsborough	3-1
Final	Burnley	Wembley	3-1

1962-63

Round 3	Burnley	(h)	0-3

1963-64

Round 3	Chelsea	(h)	1-1
Round 3 (R)	Chelsea	(a)	0-2

1964-65

Round 3	Torquay United	(a)	3-3
Round 3 (R)	Torquay United	(h)	5-1
Round 4	Ipswich Town	(h)	5-0
Round 5	Chelsea	(a)	0-1

1965-66

Round 3	Middlesbrough	(h)	4-0
Round 4	Burnley	(h)	4-3
Round 5	Preston North End	(a)	1-2

1966-67

Round 3	Milwall	(a)	0-0
Round 3 (R)	Milwall	(h)	1-0
Round 4	Portsmouth	(h)	3-1
Round 5	Bristol City	(h)	2-0
Round 6	Birmingham	(a)	0-0
Round 6 (R)	Birmingham	(h)	6-0
Semi Final	Nottingham Forest	Hillsborough	2-1
Final	Chelsea	Wembley	2-1

1967-68

Round 3	Manchester United	(a)	2-2
Round 3 (R)	Manchester United	(h)	1-0 (after extra time)
Round 4	Preston North End	(h)	3-1
Round 5	Liverpool	(h)	1-1
Round 5 (R)	Liverpool	(a)	1-2

1968-69

Round 3	Walsall	(a)	1-0
Round 4	Wolves	(h)	2-1
Round 5	Aston Villa	(h)	3-2
Round 6	Manchester City	(a)	0-1

1969-70

Round 3	Bradford City	(a)	2-2
Round 3 (R)	Bradford City	(h)	5-0
Round 4	Crystal Palace	(a)	0-1

1970-71

Round 3	Sheffield Wednesday	(h)	4-1
Round 4	Carlisle United	(a)	3-2
Round 5	Nottingham Forest	(h)	2-1
Round 6	Liverpool	(a)	0-0
Round 6 (R)	Liverpool	(h)	0-1

1971-72

Round 3	Carlisle United	(h)	1-1
Round 3 (R)	Carlisle United	(a)	3-1
Round 4	Rotherham United	(h)	2-0
Round 5	Everton	(a)	2-0
Round 6	Leeds United	(a)	1-2

1972-73

Round 3	Margate	(a)	6-0
Round 4	Derby County	(a)	1-1
Round 4 (R)	Derby County	(h)	3-5 (after extra time)

1973-74

Round 3	Leicester City	(a)	0-1

1974-75

Round 3	Nottingham Forest	(a)	1-1
Round 3 (R)	Nottingham Forest	(h)	0-1

1975-76

Round 3	Stoke City	(h)	1-1
Round 3 (R)	Stoke City	(a)	1-2

1976-77

Round 3	Cardiff City	(a)	0-1

1977-78

Round 3	Bolton Wanderers	(h)	2-2
Round 3 (R)	Bolton Wanderers	(a)	1-2 (after extra time)

1978-79

Round 3	Altrincham	(h)	1-1
Round 3 (R)	Altrincham	Maine Road	3-0
Round 4	Wrexham	(h)	3-3
Round 4 (R)	Wrexham	(a)	3-2 (after extra time)
Round 5	Oldham Athletic	(a)	1-0
Round 6	Manchester United	(h)	1-1
Round 6 (R)	Manchester United	(a)	0-2

1979-80

Round 3	Manchester United	(h)	1-1
Round 3 (R)	Manchester United	(a)	1-0 (after extra time)
Round 4	Swindon Town	(a)	0-0
Round 4 (R)	Swindon Town	(h)	2-1
Round 5	Birmingham City	(h)	3-1
Round 6	Liverpool	(h)	0-1

1980-81

Round 3	QPR	(a)	0-0
Round 3 (R)	QPR	(h)	3-1
Round 4	Hull City	(h)	2-0
Round 5	Coventry City	(h)	3-1
Round 6	Exeter City	(h)	2-0
Semi Final	Wolves	Hillsborough	2-2
Semi Final	Wolves	Highbury	3-0
Final	Manchester City	Wembley	1-1 (after extra time)
Final (R)	Manchester City	Wembley	3-2

1981-82

Round 3	Arsenal	(h)	1-0
Round 4	Leeds United	(h)	1-0
Round 5	Aston Villa	(h)	1-0
Round 6	Chelsea	(a)	3-2
Semi Final	Leicester City	Villa Park	2-0
Final	QPR	Wembley	1-1 (after extra time)
Final	QPR	Wembley	1-0

1982-83

Round 3	Southampton	(h)	1-0
Round 4	W.B.A.	(h)	2-1
Round 5	Everton	(a)	0-2

1983-84

Round 3	Fulham	(a)	0-0
Round 3 (R)	Fulham	(h)	2-0
Round 4	Norwich City	(h)	0-0
Round 4 (R)	Norwich City	(a)	1-2

1984-85

Round 3	Charlton Athletic	(h)	1-1
Round 3 (R)	Charlton Athletic	(a)	2-1
Round 4	Liverpool	(a)	0-1

1985-86

Round 3	Oxford United	(a)	1-1
Round 3 (R)	Oxford United	(h)	2-1 (after extra time)
Round 4	Notts County	(a)	1-1
Round 4 (R)	Notts County	(h)	5-0
Round 5	Everton	(h)	1-2

1986-87

Round 3	Scunthorpe United	(h)	3-2
Round 4	Crystal Palace	(h)	4-0
Round 5	Newcastle United	(h)	1-0
Round 6	Wimbledon	(a)	2-0
Semi Final	Watford	Villa Park	4-0
Final	Coventry City	Wembley	2-3 (after extra time)

1987-88

Round 3	Oldham Athletic	(a)	4-2
Round 4	Port Vale	(a)	1-2

1988-89

Round 3	Bradford City	(a)	0-1

1989-90

Round 3	Southampton	(h)	1-3

Tottenham's League Cup Record

1966-67

Round 2	West Ham United	(a)	0-1

1967-68

Did not compete

1968-69

Round 2	Aston Villa	(a)	4-1
Round 3	Exeter City	(h)	6-3
Round 4	Peterborough	(h)	1-0
Round 5	Southampton	(h)	1-0
Semi Final (1st Leg)	Arsenal	(a)	0-1
Semi Final (2nd Leg)	Arsenal	(h)	1-1 (agg 1-2)

1969-70

Round 2	Wolves	(a)	0-1

1970-71

Round 2	Swansea City	(h)	3-0
Round 3	Sheffield United	(h)	2-1
Round 4	W.B.A.	(h)	5-0
Round 5	Coventry City	(h)	4-1
Semi Final (1st Leg)	Bristol City	(a)	1-1
Semi Final (2nd Leg)	Bristol City	(h)	2-0 (after extra time, agg 3-1)
Final	Aston Villa	Wembley	2-0

1971-72

Round 2	W.B.A.	(a)	1-0
Round 3	Torquay	(a)	4-1
Round 4	Preston North End	(h)	1-1
Round 4 (R)	Preston North End	(a)	2-1 (after extra time)
Round 5	Blackpool	(h)	2-0
Semi Final (1st Leg)	Chelsea	(a)	2-3
Semi Final (2nd Leg)	Chelsea	(h)	2-2 (agg 4-5)

1972-73

Round 2	Huddersfield Town	(h)	2-1
Round 3	Middlesbrough	(a)	1-1
Round 3 (R)	Middlesbrough	(h)	0-0 (after extra time)
Round 3 (R)	Middlesbrough	(h)	2-1 (after extra time)
Round 4	Millwall	(h)	2-0
Round 5	Liverpool	(a)	1-1
Round 5 (R)	Liverpool	(h)	3-1
Semi Final (1st Leg)	Wolves	(a)	2-1
Semi Final (2nd Leg)	Wolves	(h)	2-2 (after extra time, agg 4-3)
Final	Norwich	Wembley	1-0

1973-74
Round 2   QPR   (a)   0-1

1974-75
Round 2   Middlesbrough   (h)   0-4

1975-76
Round 2   Watford   (a)   1-0
Round 3   Crewe Alexandra   (a)   2-0
Round 4   West Ham United   (h)   0-0
Round 4 (R)   West Ham United   (a)   2-0
                                                           (after
                                                           extra
                                                           time)
Round 5   Doncaster Rovers   (h)   7-2
Semi Final   Newcastle United   (h)   1-0
(1st Leg)
Semi Final   Newcastle United   (a)   1-3
(2nd Leg)   (agg 2-3)

1976-77
Round 2   Middlesbrough   (a)   2-1
Round 3   Wrexham   (h)   2-3

1977-78
Round 2   Wimbledon   (h)   4-0
Round 3   Coventry City   (h)   2-3

1978-79
Round 2   Swansea City   (a)   2-2
Round 2 (R)   Swansea City   (h)   1-3

1979-80
Round 2   Manchester United   (h)   2-1
(1st Leg)
Round 2   Manchester United   (a)   1-3
(2nd Leg)   (agg 3-4)

1980-81

Round 2 (1st Leg)	Orient	(a)	1-0
Round 2 (2nd Leg)	Orient	(h)	3-1 (agg 4-1)
Round 3	Crystal Palace	(h)	0-0
Round 3 (R)	Crystal Palace	(a)	3-1 (after extra time)
Round 4	Arsenal	(h)	1-0
Round 5	West Ham United	(a)	0-1

1981-82

Round 2 (1st Leg)	Manchester United	(h)	1-0
Round 2 (2nd Leg)	Manchester United	(a)	1-0 (agg 2-0)
Round 3	Wrexham	(h)	2-0
Round 4	Fulham	(h)	1-0
Round 5	Nottingham Forest	(h)	1-0
Semi Final (1st Leg)	W.B.A.	(a)	0-0
Semi Final (2nd Leg)	W.B.A.	(h) (h)	1-0 (agg 1-0)
Final	Liverpool	Wembley	1-3 (after extra time)

1982-83

Round 2 (1st Leg)	Brighton & HA	(h)	1-1
Round 2 (2nd Leg)	Brighton & HA	(a)	1-0 (agg 2-1)
Round 3	Gillingham	(a)	4-2
Round 4	Luton Town	(h)	1-0
Round 5	Burnley	(h)	1-4

1983-84

Round 2 (1st Leg)	Lincoln City	(h)	3-1
Round 2 (2nd Leg)	Lincoln City	(a)	1-2 (agg 4-3)
Round 3	Arsenal	(h)	1-2

1984-85

Round 2 (1st Leg)	Halifax Town	(a)	5-1
Round 2 (2nd Leg)	Halifax Town	(h)	4-0 (agg 9-1)
Round 3	Liverpool	(h)	1-0
Round 4	Sunderland	(a)	0-0
Round 4 (R)	Sunderland	(h)	1-2

1985-86

Round 2 (1st Leg)	Orient	(a)	0-2
Round 2 (2nd Leg)	Orient	(h)	4-0 (agg 4-2)
Round 3	Wimbledon	(h)	2-0
Round 4	Portsmouth	(h)	0-0
Round 4 (R)	Portsmouth	(a)	0-0 (after extra time)
Round 4 (R)	Portsmouth	(a)	0-1

1986-87

Round 2 (1st Leg)	Barnsley	(a)	3-2
Round 2 (2nd Leg)	Barnsley	(h)	5-3 (agg 8-5)
Round 3	Birmingham City	(h)	5-0
Round 4	Cambridge United	(a)	3-1
Round 5	West Ham United	(a)	1-1
Round 5 (R)	West Ham United	(h)	5-0
Semi Final (1st Leg)	Arsenal	(a)	1-0
Semi Final (2nd Leg)	Arsenal	(h)	1-2 (after extra time)
Semi Final	Arsenal	(h)	1-2

1987-88

Round 2 (1st Leg)	Torquay United	(a)	0-1
Round 2 (2nd Leg)	Torquay United	(h)	3-0 (agg 3-1)
Round 3	Aston Villa	(a)	1-2

1988-89

Round 2 (1st Leg)	Notts County	(a)	1-1
Round 2 (2nd Leg)	Notts County	(h)	2-1 (agg 3-2)
Round 3	Blackburn	(h)	0-0
Round 3 (R)	Blackburn	(a)	2-1
Round 4	Southampton	(a)	1-2

1989-90

Round 2 (1st Leg)	Southend	(h)	1-0
Round 2 (2nd Leg)	Southend	(a)	2-3 (agg 3-3) Spurs won on away goals
Round 3	Manchester United	(a)	3-0
Round 4	Tranmere	(a)	2-2
Round 4 (R)	Tranmere	(h)	4-0
Round 5	Nottingham Forest	(a)	2-2
Round 5 (R)	Nottingham Forest	(h)	2-3

Tottenham's Record in The European Cup

1961-62

Prelim Rnd (1st Leg)	Gornik Zabrze	(a)	2-4
Prelim Rnd (2nd Leg)	Gorniz Zabrze	(h)	8-1 (agg 10-5)
Round 1 (1st Leg)	Feyenoord	(a)	3-1
Round 1 (2nd Leg)	Feyenoord	(h)	1-1 (agg 4-2)
Round 2 (1st Leg)	Dukla Prague	(a)	0-1
Round 2 (2nd Leg)	Dukla Prague	(h)	4-1 (agg 4-2)
Semi Final (1st Leg)	Benfica	(a)	1-3
Semi Final (2nd Leg)	Benfica	(h)	2-1 (agg 3-4)

Tottenham's Record in The European Cup Winners' Cup

1962-63

Round 1 (1st Leg)	Glasgow Rangers	(h)	5-2
Round 1 (2nd Leg)	Glasgow Rangers	(a)	3-2 (agg 8-4)
Round 2 (1st Leg)	Slovan Bratislava	(a)	0-2
Round 2 (2nd Leg)	Slovan Bratislava	(h)	6-0 (agg 6-2)
Semi Final (1st Leg)	OFK Belgrade	(a)	2-1
Semi Final (2nd Leg)	OFK Belgrade	(h)	3-1 (agg 5-2)

1963-64

Round 1 (1st Leg)	Manchester United	(h)	2-0
Round 1 (2nd Leg)	Manchester United	(a)	1-4 (agg 3-4)

1967-68

Round 1 (1st Leg)	Hadjuk Split	(a)	2-0
Round 1 (2nd Leg)	Hadjuk Split	(h)	4-3 (agg 6-3)
Round 2 (1st Leg)	Olympique Lyonnais	(a)	0-1
Round 2 (2nd Leg)	Olympique Lyonnais	(h)	4-3 (agg 4-4)

Tottenham lose on
away goals rule

1981-82

Round 1 (1st Leg)	Ajax	(a)	3-1
Round 1 (2nd Leg)	Ajax	(h)	3-0 (agg 6-1)
Round 2 (1st Leg)	Dundalk	(a)	1-1
Round 2 (2nd Leg)	Dundalk	(h)	1-0 (agg 2-1)
Round 3 (1st Leg)	Eintracht Frankfurt	(h)	2-0
Round 3 (2nd Leg)	Eintracht Frankfurt	(a)	1-2 (agg 3-2)
Semi Final (1st Leg)	Barcelona	(h)	1-1
Semi Final (2nd Leg)	Barcelona	(a)	0-1 (agg 1-2)

1982-83

Round 1 (1st Leg)	Coleraine	(a)	3-0
Round 1 (2nd Leg)	Coleraine	(h)	4-0 (agg 7-0)
Round 2 (1st Leg)	Bayern Munich	(h)	1-1
Round 2 (2nd Leg)	Bayern Munich	(a)	1-4 (agg 2-5)

Tottenham's Record in The UEFA Cup

1971-72

Round 1 (1st Leg)	Keflavik	(a)	6-1
Round 1 (2nd Leg)	Keflavik	(h)	9-0 (agg 15-1)
Round 2 (1st Leg)	FC Nantes	(a)	0-0
Round 2 (2nd Leg)	FC Nantes	(h)	1-0 (agg 1-0)
Round 3 (1st Leg)	Rapid Bucharest	(h)	3-0
Round 3 (2nd Leg)	Rapid Bucharest	(a)	2-0 (agg 5-0)
Round 4 (1st Leg)	Unizale Textile Arad	(a)	2-0
Round 4 (2nd Leg)	Unizale Textile Arad	(h)	1-1 (agg 3-1)
Semi Final (1st Leg)	AC Milan	(h)	2-1
Semi Final (2nd Leg)	AC Milan	(a)	1-1 (agg 3-2)
Final (1st Leg)	Wolves	(a)	2-1
Final (2nd Leg)	Wolves	(h)	1-1 (agg 3-2)

1972-73

Round 1 (1st Leg)	Lyn Oslo	(a)	6-3
Round 1 (2nd Leg)	Lyn Oslo	(h)	6-0 (agg 12-3)
Round 2 (1st Leg)	Olympiakos Piraeus	(h)	4-0
Round 2 (2nd Leg)	Olympiakos Piraeus	(a)	0-1 (agg 4-1)

1972-73 (cont'd)

Round 3 (1st Leg)	Red Star Belgrade	(h)	2-0
Round 3 (2nd Leg)	Red Star Belgrade	(a)	0-1 (agg 2-1)
Round 4 (1st Leg)	Vitoria Setubal	(h)	1-0
Round 4 (2nd Leg)	Vitoria Setubal	(a)	1-2 (agg 2-2)

Tottenham win on away goals rule

Semi Final (1st Leg)	Liverpool	(a)	0-1
Semi Final (2nd Leg)	Liverpool	(h)	2-1 (agg 4-4)

Tottenham lose on away goals rule

1973-74

Round 1 (1st Leg)	Grasshoppers	(a)	5-1
Round 1 (2nd Leg)	Grasshoppers	(h)	4-1 (agg 9-2)
Round 2 (1st Leg)	Aberdeen	(a)	1-1
Round 2 (2nd Leg)	Aberdeen	(h)	4-1 (agg 5-2)
Round 3 (1st Leg)	Dynamo Tblisi	(a)	1-1
Round 3 (2nd Leg)	Dynamo Tblisi	(h)	5-1 (agg 6-2)
Round 4 (1st Leg)	Cologne	(a)	2-1
Round 4 (2nd Leg)	Cologne	(h)	3-0 (agg 5-1)

1973-74 (cont'd)

Semi Final (1st Leg)	Lokomotiv Leipzig	(a)	2-1
Semi Final (2nd Leg)	Lokomotiv Leipzig	(h)	2-0 (agg 4-1)
Final (1st Leg)	Feyenoord	(h)	2-2
Final (2nd Leg)	Feyenoord	(a)	0-2 (agg 2-4)

1983-84

Round 1 (1st Leg)	Drogheda	(a)	6-0
Round 1 (2nd Leg)	Drogheda	(h)	8-0 (agg 14-0)
Round 2 (1st Leg)	Feyenoord	(h)	4-2
Round 2 (2nd Leg)	Feyenoord	(a)	2-0 (agg 6-2)
Round 3 (1st Leg)	Bayern Munich	(a)	0-1
Round 3 (2nd Leg)	Bayern Munich	(h)	2-0 (agg 2-1)
Round 4 (1st Leg)	Austria Vienna	(h)	2-0
Round 4 (2nd Leg)	Austria Vienna	(a)	2-2 (agg 4-2)
Semi Final (1st Leg)	Hadjuk Split	(a)	1-2
Semi Final (2nd Leg)	Hadjuk Split	(h)	1-0 (agg 2-2)

Tottenham won 4-3
on penalties

1983-84 (cont'd)

Final (1st Leg)	Anderlecht	(a)	1-1
Round 2 (2nd Leg)	Anderlecht	(h)	1-1 (agg 2-2) Tottenham won 4-3 on penalties

1984-85

Round 1 (1st Leg)	Sporting Braga	(a)	3-0
Round 1 (2nd Leg)	Sporting Braga	(h)	6-0 (agg 9-0)
Round 2 (1st Leg)	Bruges	(a)	1-2
Round 2 (2nd Leg)	Bruges	(h)	3-0 (agg 4-2)
Round 3 (1st Leg)	Bohemians Prague	(h)	2-0
Round 3 (2nd Leg)	Bohemians Prague	(a)	1-1 (agg 3-1)
Round 4 (1st Leg)	Real Madrid	(h)	0-1
Round 4 (2nd Leg)	Real Madrid	(a)	0-0 (agg 0-1)